Living the Faith:
The Nicene Creed for a Postmodern Age

Gregory Hall

Living the Faith: The Nicene Creed for a Postmodern Age
ISBN: 978-1-946478-31-3 Softcover
Copyright © 2017 by Gregory Hall

All rights reserved. No part of this book may be reproduced or transmitted in any form or by any means, electronic or mechanical, including photocopying, recording, or by any information storage and retrieval system, without permission in writing from the publisher.

To order additional copies of this book, contact:

Parson's Porch Books
1-423-475-7308
www.parsonsporch.com

Parson's Porch Books is an imprint of **Parson's Porch & Book Publishers** in Cleveland, Tennessee, which has double focus. We focus on the needs of creative writers who need a professional publisher to get their work to market, **&** we also focus on the needs of others by sharing our profits with those who struggle in poverty to meet their basic needs of food, clothing, shelter and safety.

Living the Faith:
The Nicene Creed for a Postmodern Age

This dedicated to Kathleen whose support and love never fails.

And to the people of Attica, Riverside and Clarence Presbyterian Churches who have taught me so much.

Contents

Introduction 9
Chapter I 11
  We
Chapter II 18
  We Believe
Chapter III 25
  In God
Chapter IV 32
  The Triune God
Chapter V 39
  God the Father
Chapter VI 45
  The Maker
Chapter VII 51
  Fully God
Chapter VIII 58
  Fully Human
Chapter IX 64
  Suffered for Us
Chapter X 69
  Christ is Alive!
Chapter XI 75
  The Cosmic Christ
Chapter XII 81
  Christ is our Judge

Chapter XIII 86
    The Work of the Spirit
Chapter XIV 92
    Spoken Through the Prophets
Chapter XV 98
    One, Holy, Catholic and Apostolic Church
Chapter XVI 104
    The Gift of Forgiveness
Chapter XVII 110
    Life in the World to Come
Chapter XVIII 116
    Conclusion

Introduction

We are living in a difficult time for Mainline Protestant Christians. For more than fifty years the signs of institutional health have all been negative. We have seen a decline in numbers in worship, money, quality of leadership and probably what has been most painful of all the loss of cultural significance.

There have been so many changes that have contributed to these crises. This post-modern, post-Christendom reality has posed challenges to the wider Christian community at all levels.

There have been all kinds of responses to the problems besetting the church. All kinds of people have tried to provide some great program that will turn things around. People have developed the "surefire marketing strategy" that bends the demographic trajectory. Others have suggested that contemporary music in worship will make all the difference. For others, it is small groups that is the answer. But the reality is there is no magic bullet.

I believe that we are living in a time of fundamental change. This is a time of fundamental change as important as the reformation and the enlightenment. In times of such transformational change it is important to look at the core meaning and practice of the faith. It is only by reconnecting to the power of the core teaching of the faith that we can begin to re-engineer how we do church.

The most fundamental of all Christian understandings is found in the creed developed by the Christian Church in the fourth century. This creed developed over many years at two ecumenical councils (325 AD and 381 AD) is called the Nicene Creed. It is shared by almost all Christians across time and space. It serves as basic understanding of the Christian movement.

> We believe in one God, the Father, the Almighty, maker of heaven and earth, of all that is, seen and unseen.
>
> We believe in one Lord, Jesus Christ, the only Son of God, eternally begotten of the Father, God from God, Light from

Light, true God from true God, begotten, not made, of one Being with the Father; through him all things were made. For us and for our salvation he came down from heaven, was incarnate of the Holy Spirit and the Virgin Mary and became truly human. For our sake, he was crucified under Pontius Pilate; he suffered death and was buried. On the third day, he rose again in accordance with the Scriptures; he ascended into heaven and is seated at the right hand of the Father. He will come again in glory to judge
The living and the dead, and his kingdom will have no end.

We believe in the Holy Spirit, the Lord, the giver of life, who proceeds from the Father and the Son, who with the Father and the Son is worshiped and glorified, who has spoken through the prophets. We believe in one holy catholic and apostolic church. We acknowledge one baptism for the forgiveness of sins. We look for the resurrection of the dead, and the life of the world to come. Amen.

I invite you to explore with me the meaning of this most basic and fully ecumenical understanding of the faith as found in the Creed. We will approach this creed one word or phrase at a time. There are questions at the end of each chapter that I invite you to pause and ponder its meaning for you and the church.

Chapter I

We

For it seemed good to the Holy Spirit and to us to lay upon you no greater burden than these necessary things.
                                                                                    Acts 15:28

One of the most intriguing book titles I have come across was **"The Unauthorized Guide to Choosing a Church"** by Carmen Berry. In this book Berry seeks to give advice from her experience to people who have no church affiliation and are seeking a church home. She shares her reasons for returning to a faith community in these words:

> **When a friend committed suicide, I realized I could become too cynical, too lost and too alone. I needed a church, a community of believers. I needed to live in my faith and visit my doubts. Something happens there that simply doesn't when you are alone in prayer or on the internet.**

Berry had discovered a central truth about our faith. Christianity is not a solitary journey but rather a shared pilgrimage. You and I need each other in our search for God. How are we to be guided in this shared journey? I believe that the Nicene Creed can shape our common life.

The Nicene Creed like most of the early creeds began in a controversy. In the early fourth century, Arius, a priest in Alexandria, made a simple statement about the God head. He said, "there was a time when the Son was not." He was saying that God the Father existed before God the Son. This struck many people as meaning that the Son was not fully divine and if the Son was not fully divine then Jesus could not be the Savior.

In very short order people took up sides. This controversy threatened to destroy the unity of the church. The Emperor became so concerned about the level of disagreement that he encouraged the

Bishops of the Church to gather together to find some compromise. So, in 325 A.D. Bishops from around the world gathered in Nicea to find a solution. They wrote a creed, which was rewritten some fifty years later, which has come to be called the Nicene Creed.

What was the function of the creed? All too often we act as if the purpose of the early creeds of the church was to lay out every detail of Christian understanding. We sometimes approach these statements as out lining exactly what God is like. It can seem like these are declarations of complete truth.

But I do not think they are to function in that manner. The Creeds are to function as maps or sign posts on our journeys towards God. They are not ultimate truth themselves, but rather point us to where truth might be found. Two years ago, Diana Butler Bass wrote a book called **"Christianity After Religion."** In this book, we find these words:

> **"I don't want to be part of your church, because I don't believe in the Nicene Creed" is a common objection of those considering Christianity- or those considering leaving Christianity. But Christians do not worship a creed. The Nicene Creed was written some three centuries after Jesus taught his followers to love God and their neighbors. For the first three hundred years of church history the followers of Jesus worshipped God, served others, preached, taught, baptized and evangelized the world without the benefit of a formal, universal doctrinal statement. The creeds developed in the context of a living, transformative, prayer-filled, risky, and active spiritual life- not the other way around. Indeed, a creed is considered a "symbol of faith, not the faith itself. The words function as an icon, a linguistic picture of a divine reality beyond the ideas and concepts, a window into the world beyond words. Creeds are not unimportant; they are important only in the right orders.**

In this study, we are going to explore where this ancient creed is pointing us in our Christian journey, and the first sign post is the simple word WE. The creed begins with the first-person plural. This reminds us that Christianity is not a solitary journey-it is a communal experience. For Christians truth is found in a shared journey of discovery.

What I have just said can sometimes be painful for Americans to hear. It is counter cultural to say that truth is corporate. We Americans have built a culture that considers individual tastes and preferences to be our highest value. Robert Bellah wrote a famous study of the uniquely American way of viewing the world in a book called **"Habits of the Heart"** In the book we find these words:

> **Individualism lies at the very core of American culture. Every one of the four traditions we have singled out is in a profound sense individualistic. There is a biblical individualism and a civic individualism as well as a utilitarian and an expressive individualism. Whatever the differences among the traditions and the consequent differences in their understanding of individualism, there are some things they all share, things that are basic to American identity. We believe in the dignity, indeed the sacredness of the individual. Anything that would violate our right to think for ourselves, judge for ourselves, make our own decisions, live our lives as we see fit, is not only morally wrong, it is sacrilegious.**

I think Bellah is fundamentally correct. I know that when I think about politics, art or religion it is through the lens of individualism. I believe that this lens of individualism makes it difficult for us to understand the Church as being more than a collection of individuals. Salvation becomes only a personal experience of Christ. The truth of the faith is reduced to my opinion. When this is taken to the extreme we become cut off from each other and the great tradition of the Church. When we only say this is what I believe we can become little Gods unto ourselves.

Bellah gives us an extreme example of this tendency in his chapter on religion. He writes:

One person we interviewed has named her religion (she calls it her faith) after herself. This suggests the logical possibility of over 220 million American religions, one for each of us. Shelia Larson is a young nurse who describes her faith as "Sheilaism." "I believe in God, I'm not a religious fanatic. I can't remember the last time I went to Church. My faith has carried me a long way. It is Shelaism. Just my own little voice." Sheila's faith has some tenets beyond belief in God, though not many. In defining "my own Sheilaism", she said: "It's just trying to love yourself and be gentle with yourself. You know, I guess take care of each other. I think He would want us to take care of each other." Like many others, Sheila would be willing to endorse few more specific injunctions.

The description of Shelaism may cause us to laugh. But are we all that much different? Do we not create our own personal system of beliefs without being accountable to others? Many times, we create our faith as if we were ordering from a Chinese menu. I will take one from Column A and two from Column B and so on. We think that we can find the truth using our own personal reason and experience. Our faith is our personal faith, it is our property. We do not need any other person to tell us what it is all about.

This extreme form of individualism is so much in the air we breathe that we think this is the way it has always been. It is so prevalent that we find it hard even to recognize. We act as if there is no other way to approach faith except as an individual quest.

The followers of Jesus had received the Holy Spirit at Pentecost. Notice this happened when they are gathered together in one place. This event had given them the courage to begin to share the good news of Jesus' resurrection with the world.

At first, they limited themselves to fellow Jews. They took their message that the Messiah had come to the synagogues. In many ways, they continued to believe that they were good Jews who knew that the Old Testament prophecies concerning the coming Messiah had been fulfilled in Jesus. The gift of eternal life had come in the raising of Jesus from death. The first Jewish Christians continued to worship in the synagogues. They continued to keep kosher dietary laws; in short, they continued to be good observant Jews.

Then something strange began to happen. Gentiles began to become attracted to Jesus. They were excited by the news of Jesus' victory over death. They wanted to share in the forgiveness of sins and the hope of eternal life. They wanted to know Jesus' love and acceptance.

The question to be decided was what should the church do with Gentiles? Did they first have to become Jews to be followers of Jesus? There were many leaders in the Christian movement who said yes. They felt that to be a follower of Jesus, male Gentiles would have to be circumcised. It would mean Gentile households would have to become kosher. It would mean that every rule developed by the Rabbi's would apply to Christians.

There were others, such as Paul, who rejected this notion. They believed that Jesus' coming into the world represented a new beginning. They believed that his coming meant the law was fulfilled and that Jesus was a new lawgiver who brought freedom from the old ways.

It is important to notice that the church did not split over this issue. Paul did not say, "I have the whole truth, if you do not follow my way, I will cease to consider you a follower of Jesus." James did not reject Paul as being a heretic who should not even be listened to for leadership or advice. They did not even say each should go their own way.

No, leaders from this new Christian movement gathered in Jerusalem to thrash out the issue. In the Book of Acts we find an event that is called the first ecumenical council. Representatives from the various factions of the Church met together, studied together, argued together, ate together and prayed together.

They knew that individually they did not have a corner on the truth. They knew that they needed each other to discover God's will. They believed that the Holy Spirit would guide them into a deeper relationship with God. The result of the Council was neither a rejection of the Old Testament nor a demand that all Gentiles become Jews.

The Council decided that baptism was the mark of a Christian not circumcision. The Ten Commandments were still binding on Christians but not the dietary laws. They began to share their findings with other Christians in these words **for it seemed good to the Holy Spirit and to us to lay upon you no greater burden than these necessary things.**

This became the pattern for seeking truth in the Church. It was understood that the Holy Spirit works in community to guide the church. The Christian faith is not our personal property. It is not our opinion. No one person has the corner on the truth.

The truth of God is found in community. We need each other to help discover the truth that God would share with us. When we stand to recite the Creed; we join our voices with all Christians across time and space. It does not mean that each one of us understands and accepts every word of the Creed. It does mean we affirm the guidance of all those past and present who have sought the love of Jesus.

In some ways, the most important word in the Nicene Creed is the first –WE

When we stand and say, "we believe" we are united with Christians in the past

With new Christians baptized in the catacombs in Rome

With Bishops meeting at Nicea

With Calvin and Luther who sought to reform the church

When we say we believe, we affirm our unity today.

With Christians from Iraq and Syria struggling to find safety amidst war

With Chinese Christians in house churches fearful of being arrested

And with our Christian brothers and sisters from different Christian traditions who live next door to us.

Yes, when we say **We Believe**, the Creed unites us with every Christian around the world today and every believer who came before us who now surround the throne of heaven.

Questions to ponder

> 1. Do I only think of Christianity as my faith rather than our faith?
> 2. Is truth personal or corporate or both?
> 3. Have I been able to learn from others with whom I disagree?

Prayer

Loving and community building God, teach me to seek your truth in community. Give me an open spirit that I might learn from others. Help me support your Church as she seeks to follow you in discovering wisdom for the journey. Amen.

Chapter II

We Believe

But I am not ashamed, for I know whom I have believed, and I am sure that he is able to guard until that day what has been entrusted to me.

II Timothy 1:12

If I were asked to provide a reading list of books to help someone understand the political and intellectual history of the 20th Century there is no doubt that the first book on the list would be **Witness**. **Witness** was written by Whittaker Chambers whose experience reflected many of the central issues of the last century. In beautiful prose, Chambers traces his experience beginning with his birth in 1901. Chambers grew up in a middle-class family. Following high school, he studied at Columbia. He became attracted to the promise of the newly formed Soviet Union. He became a member of the communist party for ten years. He did espionage work for the Soviets during the 1930's. He left the party in 1938 and became a Senior Editor at Time Magazine. During this time, he became a Christian.

In subsequent years, he became famous as the chief witness against Alger Hiss, a high official in the State Department, who was convicted of spying for the Soviet Union in 1948. **Witness** is Chambers' reflections on his life and its meaning for history. In the preface, he spoke of the crises that faced Western Culture. He wrote:

> **Economics is not the central problem of this century; it is a relative problem that can be solved in relative ways. Faith is the central problem of this age. The western world does not know it, but it already possesses the answer to this problem- but only provided that its faith in God and the freedom He enjoins is as great as Communism's faith in man.**

I believe that in some ways Chamber's observations are still true today. We live in a culture experiencing a crisis in faith. People wonder what is true? What should I believe? What is more, we live in a time when the Christian church is struggling with the meaning of belief.

In this chapter, we focus on the second word of the Nicene Creed. At first hearing or reading we think we know what this word means. During the last two hundred years Protestant Christians have understood the word believe to mean giving intellectual assent to certain propositions about God.

Following the reformation, the enlightenment and the rise of modern science and abstract scholarship, the Christian faith was largely understood to be a set of ideas about God. Belief therefore was defined as affirming a prescribed set of propositions about the divine.

It is no surprise that for decade's youth would go through a confirmation program in their church and then often would disappear. They stood before the congregation and declared their belief in a set of ideas about God, end of story. They had done what was expected of them. They affirmed the right set of words about God, there was nothing more to do. This is the result of a narrow modern understanding of what it means to say, "we believe."

Diana Butler Bass reminds us of the Christian history related to the concept of belief in these words:

> "To believe" in Latin (the shaping language for much of Western theological thought) is opinor, meaning "opinion", which was not typically a religious word. Instead, Latin used credo, "I set my heart upon" or "I give my loyalty to," as the word to describe religious "believing" that is "faith." In medieval English, the concept of credo was translated as "believe" meaning roughly the same thing as its German cousin "belieben", "to prize, treasure, or hold dear," which come from the root word meaning love. Thus, in early English, to "believe" was to "belove" something or

someone as an act or trust or loyalty. Belief was not an intellectual opinion.

In previous centuries, belief had nothing to do with one's weighing of evidence or intellectual choice. Believe was not a doctrinal test. Instead, belief was more like a marriage vow- "I do" as a pledge of faithfulness and loving service to and with the other. Indeed, in early English usage, you could not hold claim, or possess a belief about God, but you could cherish, love, trust in, or devote yourself to God.

Given all this, what do we mean when we stand to affirm a creed and we declare- We believe?

First, it means we are promising to use the words of the creed as a guide in our seeking to discover God. The words of the creed do not completely describe God, but they are reliable sign posts or a map that points the way for us to discover the truths of God.

One of my friends in college had a Peanuts poster on her wall which read: **It does not matter what I believe as long as I am sincere!**

This could not be further from the truth. The quality of our belief is not determined by the emotion we put behind it. The value of our belief is not determined by the earnestness in holding our belief. No, the quality is determined by the object of our belief.

What do I mean by this? Well, it does not matter how determinedly you might believe that you can jump off the Empire State building and fly on your own power, it won't happen. You can have all the sincerity in the world and you still end up a spot on the sidewalk.

What is crucial is not the intensity of our faith, but rather the truth of the object. We have a great faith because God is real and has revealed God's self to us in Jesus. The words of the Nicene Creed serve as a faithful guide for our discovery of the truth of God. Thus, when we say, "We Believe", it means we affirm the words of the Creed as pointing the way for us to find the meaning of God and his love for us. The Creed helps to guide our minds.

A second meaning of our declaring "We believe" is that we are committing ourselves to interpreting the world through a Christian understanding of reality.

Each human being is trained in or chooses a unique lens through which to look at and understand the world. We each make certain assumptions concerning how the world works and understand events through that framework. Facts are facts, but how we understand them, how we put them together is determined by our view of the world.

One example of this is the perpetual enigma of history as to whether Napoleon was a great liberator of Europe or a power-mad conqueror; he has been seen both ways by his contemporaries and by historians. Judging whether he was one or the other largely depends on the world view of the observer.

In the last 100 years there have been many competing world views in the west. As Chambers so vividly wrote, Marxism captured the imagination and hearts of millions of people around the world. Marxism was an ideology that sought to understand the world through the lens of economic relationships. All of reality from politics to family life was understood to be governed by economics. This led to people interpreting the events of the world and their lives through the lens of Marxism.

Another favorite lens of interpreting life in our time has been psychology. Since the time of Freud our culture had been fascinated with the human mind and how it works. We have sought explanations of human behavior in childhoods and the unconscious. Just think of how often we remove responsibility from people who have committed reproachable acts by saying something about their parents.

There is some truth in Marxism, there is truth in Freud and there is truth is some of the other lenses people have used to seek to understand the world. The problem is that they are not large enough to understand all truth. They are all limited.

The lens that Christians are called to use to understand the world is our Christian faith. The truth found in Scripture, Creed and tradition help serve to illuminate the world for us. When we want to know the meaning of creation we look to God the Father. When we want to understand what it means to be fully human we look to the picture of Jesus painted in the Gospels. When we want to comprehend the nature of love, we ponder the cross of Christ.

So, when we stand and say we believe- we are promising that we will seek to understand reality informed by the Creed's presentation of truth. A meaning of belief is to allow the truth of God to shape our view of the world.

Finally, the statement "We believe" has a personal component. When we join our voices with others in saying we believe- we are making a decision to become one with Christ and his church. We are affirming our identity as followers of Jesus. The deepest and most profound meaning of the words We Believe is that we are saying that the God pointed to by the creed is the one we trust with our very being.

The decision for or against Christ is one each one of us makes for ourselves in the privacy of our hearts and minds. You and I are not Christians because Mom or Dad went to Church. We are not believers because we are born in America. We are followers of Jesus when we give our trust to God enough to put him at the center of our lives.

Do not worry about the strength of your faith. It may be weak or strong at any point in time. There are times when our faith seems so assured and God is very real to us. There are other times when our faith seems weak and God can seem to be in hiding. Do not despair. The power of our faith does not come from within us. Its effectiveness does not come from our internal strength. No, the power of our faith comes from its object which is Jesus himself.

When we were quite young, by sister and I had a small record player. For those who are younger, before smart phones, before IPODs, before CD' S and before tapes, the way we listened to music was on records made out of vinyl. We had several small records with one song on each side call 45's.

These old 45's had a large hole in the middle. This meant you had to place a special adapter on the turntable in order to hold the record in place. I remember that one time we lost the adapter and we tried to play the record without it. Time and again I tried to place the record exactly centered on the turn table, I would then gently place the needle on the record. After several measures of music, the record revolving would move off center and the needle would slide off the turntable. The adapter was needed to hold the record on center. Without something solidly at the center of the 45 holding it in place is could not function.

I believe that you and I are similar to those old 45's. We need to have something we trust at the very core of our lives. We need God at the center of our lives to hold our lives together.

In 1921 William Butler Yeats published a poem called "The Second Coming." Ireland was suffering from the aftermath of World War I and the Easter Rebellion. The recent events had shattered the idealism of the previous century. Yeats wrote a line which has haunted the last 100 years.

Things fall apart; the center cannot hold.

Friends we have a center that can hold. Jesus Christ came to reveal God's love for us. In life and death, we can trust in God's love. We can build our lives upon the rock of salvation. When we say, "we believe", we center our lives on God.

Questions to ponder

    1. What has been your definition of believe?
    2. How are trust and belief related in your understanding?
    3. Have you put God at the center of your life?

Prayer

Gracious God who gives us life and being. You have gifted us with minds that reach out to you seeking understanding. Remind us that we can never fully grasp all knowledge. Teach us that we cannot wait for all things to be proven before putting our trust in you. Encourage us to give our hearts to you knowing that this will lead to a deeper wisdom. Amen

Chapter III

In God

No one has ever seen God; the only Son, who is in the bosom of the Father, he has made him known.
                                                           John 1:18

One of the recipients of the Templeton Prize for Progress in Religion was Michael Novak. Novak was a teacher, philosopher and a onetime US diplomat. He is known as the author of many scholarly works. But not long after receiving the Templeton award, Novak published a more popular work. The book had the title *Tell Me Why: A Father Answers His Daughter's Questions About God*. This book is a record of the written correspondence between Novak and his adult daughter.

Early in the book Jana asks this question:

> **After all, in this age of advanced technology and knowledge, when the need for god or gods to explain the unexplainable is seemingly unnecessary, how can one believe in God? It seems difficult to find a reason for god- let alone to prove he exists.**

I believe that Jana speaks for many people today. There are many men and women who find the hardest aspect of Christianity to accept is the reality of God. When they read the stories in the New Testament they find Jesus to be an attractive figure. The accounts of his interactions with common people, his parables and stories paint a winsome picture. Jesus' teaching in the Sermon on the Mount make people want to be better people. The model of the Church described in the Book of Acts is a community many would like to follow.

The whole system of Christian belief is something many people would like to accept if only...if only they could believe in God.

It is not so much that people are virulently atheistic. There are not many Christopher Hitchens or Dawkins around who want to stamp out every reference to the divine. There are relatively few people who are hostile to the idea of God. There are just many people who struggle to believe or who leave the question with a shrug and an "I don't know."

In his novel **A Farewell to Arms,** Earnest Hemingway has someone ask Lieutenant Henry, who was wounded in the First World War, if he is croyant- that is if he is a believer. **"Only at night," he replies. In the daytime when his mind is alert, he can no longer believe; at night, some of the old yearnings return."**

There are so many people who harbor a sad reluctant agnosticism. People who wish the Christian faith were true, yet can't quite cross the threshold to faith.

One major reason that people find it hard to believe in God is because they have been taught that science has taken the place of God. This happens in many ways. People have come to think that science gives explanations that religion used to provide.

In the congregation, I served in the village of Attica, NY, there was a teenage boy who was taking biology in high school. He came home from class one day and told his mother he no longer needed God because biology explained how nature operated. This young man believed the entire purpose of God was to explain the unexplainable. Since the rise of modern science there have been many people who have understood God in this manner.

Many of the early scientists misused God in this way. One example is Isaac Newton. According to Newton's calculations, there were slight irregularities in the orbits of the planets which would in time cause the solar system to collapse. Newton believed that unless those irregularities were corrected by divine intervention, the solar system could not continue indefinitely. This was but one of several things that Newton taught that God needed to do to keep the machine of the created order in balance.

The God of the scientists became known as the "God of the Gaps." This meant that whenever science could not discover an answer to a question, God became the solution to the gap of knowledge. As science could answer more and more questions the gap became smaller and smaller. When the famous French Scientist Pierre Laplace published a book on celestial mechanics, Napoleon complained that Laplace had neglected to mention God. Laplace coolly replied, "Sir, I have no need for that hypothesis."

A second way in which science leads to agnosticism is that the success of modern science has led many people to believe that the only truth is that which can be discovered through the scientific method. It is science alone that is the arbiter of truth. Most of us have been raised to believe that the only truth that is real is that which can be measured.

Now the very nature of the Christian understanding of the divine puts God outside the natural world. God cannot be grasped by our senses. God cannot be measured by science. Science can only deal with the physical creation, since God is not part of the created order, he cannot be discovered by science.

For a long time these concepts have made it difficult for many people to seriously entertain the possibility of God. The Bible does not argue for the existence of God, it does not give proofs for God; it takes belief in a supreme being for granted. The Bible reveals the nature of God, not God's reality.

In the last forty years the hostility to the idea of God has begun to soften. Today there have been fundamental developments in philosophy and cosmology that point to God. These changes do not prove God's existence but rather can open us to the possibility of God.

First, the mere existence of the world points to the possibility of God. The fact that this universe exists causes us to begin to ask questions. We wonder, how did this world come to be? It must have come from somewhere? It must have some purpose?

These are questions that are being wrestled with today at the highest level of physics. Paul Davies is a British physicist who has taught at several universities in Britain, the US and Australia He is another winner of the Templeton prize. In his address on accepting the prize we find these words:

> **Now you might think I have written God entirely out of the picture. Who needs a God when the laws of physics can do such a splendid job? But we are bound to return to that burning question: Where do the laws of physics come from? Most especially: Why a set of laws that drives the searing, featureless gases coughed out of the big bang toward life and consciousness and intelligence and cultural activities such as religion, art mathematics, and science?**

Remember this is not a preacher talking, this is a physicist. The mere fact of existence opens to us the possibility of God.

Secondly, the order of creation points towards God.

There are two interesting facts that the study of nature teaches us. The first is that the universe has an order. Science, from the time of the Greeks until today, has sought to discover how nature operates with a belief that there are laws which govern the operation of the universe. The goals of biology, chemistry and physics are, through observation and experiment, to uncover these rules. Galileo discovered the laws governing falling bodies by dropping different weights from a great height. Science seeks to discover the order which governs the creation.

Yet science also teaches us that the present order is not the only possible order. Nature could have been ordered in a different way. The laws of gravity could be different.

The ancient Greeks were limited in their scientific discoveries in part because they were so closely wedded to abstract reason. Many Greeks attempted to discover how nature worked from the top down. That is, they assumed all the laws of nature were derived from an abstract balanced mathematical ideal.

The great discoveries of modern science have come from the bottom up. From observing nature itself. The operation of nature is reasonable, but often it is not what we would expect. There is an order and balance in the natural world, yet it is not the only order possible. Thus, we begin to ask the question, "Why this order?"

This question is one, which fascinates many physicists. Realizing that just the slightest changes in the way the universe was put together would have made conscious human life impossible, Paul Davies says:

> **The fact that the universe is as it is, in particular the laws permit the emergence of conscious beings that can reflect the meaning of it all, is surely a fact of immense significance. What never ceases to surprise me and fill me with awe and wonder is the mounting evidence that we are truly meant to be here.**

In recent decades physicists have noticed an astonishing thing about the fundamental laws of nature. The 20 or so parameters they contain-numbers governing the strength of gravity, the ratio of the proton's size to the neutron's and so on-appear to have been fine-tuned so that, against astronomically unfavorable odds, conscious organisms could emerge. Make gravity the slightest bit weaker, and no galaxies suitable for the life would have formed; make it the slightest bit stronger and the cosmos would have collapsed upon itself moments after the big bang. The universe, as astronomer Fred Hoyle once remarked, looks like a put-up job, who but a Divine Designer could have twiddled with these 20 different "control knobs" until they were pointing at precisely the right values for the full array of life to appear.

Hoyle who was one of the progenitors of the term "big bang", spoke of the possibility of a designer of the universe when he said, **an explosion in a junkyard does not lead to sundry bits of metal being assembled into a useful working machine.**

I believe that the fact the world exists and in this order points to a divine intelligence with a purpose at work in creation.

I believe that you and I are living in a time when the false barriers to a belief in God are falling. The intellectual walls that kept many people from integrating their faith and their minds are crumbling. We again can allow the natural world to point us towards God. We can allow the various experiences of our lives to lead us toward the divine.

The poet Christopher Frye speaks of the new openness in these words:

> **The Frozen misery**
> **Of centuries breaks, cracks, begins to move,**
> **The thunder is the thunder of the floes,**
> **The thaw, the flood, the upstart of Spring.**
> **The longest stride of soul men ever took.**
> **Affairs are now soul size,**
> **The enterprise is exploration into God**

Friends, when we affirm that we believe in God, we join a great journey. While we do not have all the answers, we become part of an exploration into God. In this life, we will not be able to know all that we would like for we seek to know the God who is not of this world.

No one has ever seen God; the only Son, who is in the bosom of the Father, he has made him known.

> **Affairs are now soul size,**
> **The enterprise is exploration into God**

Questions

> 1. Have you at any time believed in the "God of the gaps?"
> 2. What do you see as the relationship between science and faith?
> 3. Have you gone through a time when a belief in God seemed unreasonable?

Prayer

Hidden God, the creator of this world yet not a part of the created order. We can only speak in pictures and metaphors about your being. Yet so often we have tried to shape you into the answers to our questions or the provider for our needs. Open our hearts and minds that we might discover new truths about you which are more wondrous than we can imagine. Amen

Chapter IV

The Triune God

All that the Father has is mine, therefore I said that he will take what is mine and declare it to you.
                                                                    John 16:15

I baptize you in the name of the Father, Son and Holy Spirit. These words have been pronounced millions of times over the heads of infants and adults for two millennia.

Go forth into the world in peace and May the blessing of God, the Father, Son and Holy Spirit be upon you and remain with you always... has been proclaimed at the end of Christian worship services for nearly two thousand years.

So far in our study we have focused on the first several words of the creed. We looked at "we" and "believe" and "in God." In this chapter, we look at the structure of the creed. The creed seeks to tell us about the nature of God in three sections. The words Father, Son and Holy Spirit indicate a basic teaching of the Christian faith about the nature of God. The first part of the creed is called the first article and talks about God the Father. The second article talks of God the Son and the third article speaks of the Holy Spirit. One of the primary teachings of the creed is the triune nature of God. We believe that God is both one and three. There is one God, but three persons.

Now I know some of you reading this may find your eyes are starting to glaze over. At first reading the idea of the Trinity seems unrelated to our daily experience. Please bear with me. I know this can be confusing material for us to wrestle with.

I should begin by acknowledging that the idea of the Trinity is indeed a deep mystery. There is an old joke that a preacher told her congregation that the problem with the Trinity is that if you don't believe it you risk losing your soul, but if you try to explain it you risk losing your mind.

The Doctrine of the Trinity seeks to comprehend the incomprehensible and to describe the indescribable. This doctrine attempts to probe the depth of the mystery of God. It proclaims the paradox that God is both one and three. It declares that at the very heart of the Godhead there are three persons, yet they are so bound together in love that they are one. Our minds tell us that God must either be one or three, yet the paradox of our faith is that God is one in three and three in one.

Thus, you might ask, "Why even talk about the Trinity?" Why should we think about a dusty old teaching from 1700 years ago composed by a bunch of men who spoke Greek and Latin? Thomas Jefferson called the Doctrine of the Trinity "gibberish." We might be led to believe that the Doctrine of the Trinity is a museum piece that has no real relevance for us living in the 21st century.

I believe that the Trinity is a core life-giving teaching about the nature of God. I believe this doctrine teaches profound truths about the nature of reality. The teaching about the Triune God is a foundational teaching that helps us to understand the rest of the Christian faith. The meaning of creation and the reality of the incarnation are informed by our understanding of God as three in one. Indeed, the Passion of Jesus is informed by a Trinitarian understanding. When we understand that there are three persons united in love, then Jesus' death on the cross is nothing less that the tearing apart of the very heart of God.

In addition to its importance in Christian Doctrine, the Trinity has practical implications for our everyday lives. The Trinity informs our everyday lives in a profound way.

The Doctrine of the Trinity does nothing less than teach us the meaning of love. The Christian understanding of love is defined by the relationship of the Father, Son and Holy Spirit. The Bible teaches us that God is love. The meaning of that love is found in the relationship between the Father, Son and Spirit.

This Doctrine tells us that love begins by recognizing the reality of others. In the Trinity there are three persons, Father, Son and Holy

Spirit. These are real entities. This Doctrine does not teach us that God wears three masks. God does not put on the Father mask at one time and then a different mask at other times. There is no God behind the persons. The persons of the Trinity are different from one another. They are unique persons.

Love begins with the recognition that there are people and things that have a reality apart from us. This is part of the meaning of the beautiful words in Genesis "God beheld his creation and said it is very good." God observes the creation and says, it is good just the way it is, not just in relationship to me but good in and of itself. It has independent value.

In her novel **The Unicorn,** Iris Murdock describes a character by the name of Effingham Cooper. Through a series of events he ends up alone stranded in a bog. He begins to sink and it becomes clear to him that he is helpless and is going to die. At first, he panics, but then a calm comes over him and he experiences a tremendous love for creation itself. He loved the beauty and wonder of the created order, a beauty that he realizes will exist even when he is gone. He loves creation apart from his own existence.

You and I can experience the same thing in small ways. Have you ever watched some young children at play? They may be children you do not know but you are just glad that they are alive and enjoying themselves. You may have smiled and felt a sense of gratitude for them merely existing. You are happy for them just being who they are.

A love grounded in the Trinity begins by recognizing the reality of others and yet preserving the bond of unity. All too often we believe that love means being the same. We feel that the unity can only be maintained if we are the same. The love of the Trinity teaches us that we can be one and yet two. All our loves must be shaped by this truth.

The Trinity is the model for our love of the created order. Our love for nature itself must be one in which we accept the reality of the created order apart from ourselves. For much of western history, human beings have seen the unity between nature and humankind as being one in which the created order has been made to submit to our will.

This lack of respect has led to polluted rivers and lakes and smog alerts. In places on the earth we have threatened our own health because we have failed to respect the truth that nature is separate from us. We have failed to love nature with a divine love. A true environmental movement is one that acts in love towards the created order. It sees that nature has a life and purpose of its own. This will teach us to respect its uniqueness and care for it.

Romantic love needs to be patterned on the Trinity. The story of Romeo and Juliet is a story in which this is forgotten. Their romance is a push towards unity. The differences between the Montagues and the Capulets must be obliterated in the search for unity. They finally could accomplish this unity only in death, death which destroys their individuality and allows them to become one.

Romantic love grounded in the Trinity does not find its unity by destroying the personalities of the two people involved.

In his book **The Road Less Traveled**, Scott Peck talks of marriage being like a base camp for mountain climbers. Climbers need a base camp. Successful mountain climbers know that they must spend as much time, if not more tending to their base camp as they do in climbing mountains. Their survival is dependent upon their seeing to it that their base camp is sturdily constructed and well stocked. Yet climbers must also leave the camp to conquer the mountain.

There is a unity in marriage. Romantic love calls us to nurture and care for our partner. Yet each person also must go out on his or her own individual journey. Male and female both tend the hearth and venture forth. Marriage is to be a unity of two people. They remain two unique individuals held together by a bond of love. Romantic love modeled on the Trinity allows us to be individuals and yet united in a bond that cannot be broken.

Parental love needs to be modeled on the love found in the Godhead. All too often the unity that is found in families is founded on submission to the will of the dominant parent. Sometimes it is the Father and sometimes it is the Mother.

We have all known families in which one of the parents is a tyrant. Their will, whims and wishes are law. There often is a unity that is enforced by fear. We have met parents who fail to acknowledge the unique individuality of their children. They regard their children as extensions of themselves in much the same way as their clothes or manicured lawns represent their status to the world.

This leads to predictable results. Either the child maintains an identity by rebelling and disrupting the family, or the child submits and has his or her will and personality shrunken or destroyed.

A love rooted in the Trinity realizes that unity comes from caring for the other and building up one who is separate from you. A child is unique in his or her own right and needs nurture and care. The unity of parental love matures with respect for the uniqueness of others.

The Poet Gibran captures this picture of parental love modeled on the Trinity in these words:

> **Your children are not your children.**
> **They are the sons and daughters of Life's longing for itself.**
> **They come through you but not from you,**
> **And though they are with you, yet they belong not to you.**
> **You may give them your love but not your thoughts.**
> **For they have their own thoughts.**
> **You may house their bodies but not their souls,**
> **For their souls dwell in the house of tomorrow, which you cannot visit, not even in your dreams.**
> **You may strive to be like them, but seek not to make them like you.**
> **For life goes not backward nor tarries with yesterday.**
> **You are the bows from which your children as living arrows are sent forth.**

> The archer sees the mark upon the path of the infinite, and He bends you with His might that His arrows may go swift and far.
> Let your bending in the archer's hand be for gladness; For even as He loves the arrow that flies, so He loves also the bow that is stable.

This is Trinitarian love. A love that respects differences and builds each other up is not natural. In this fallen world, we tend either to let our differences divide and separate us, or we seek to obliterate the differences.

We need to be reminded that in the very core of reality, in the very heart of God is difference. Ultimate realty is not moving towards a unity which erases all differences. Ultimate reality is found in the community of the Father, Son and Holy Spirit. Our personalities, our uniqueness has ultimate value. Our eternal destiny is to become part of the divine community where we share in that love which binds all things together.

The Doctrine of the Trinity is not some relic of a bygone era.
It is a living truth that shapes our lives and loves
It can help us learn how to love our spouses
And our children
And our neighbors

We believe in the Father, Son and Holy Spirit.

Questions

>   1. Can you live with the paradox that God is both three and one?
>   2. Do you resonate primarily with the oneness or Threeness in God?
>   3. Does it surprise you that the trinity is the model for marriage and parenting?

Prayer

Triune God, your nature is beyond our understanding. Help us to cherish the tension of the truth that you are both one and three. Help us to ground all our loves in that love which holds the Godhead in one. Teach us to love others without seeking to erase our differences. Amen

Chapter V

God the Father

For you did not receive the spirit of slavery to fall back into fear, but you have received the spirit of Sonship. When we cry, "Abba! Father!" is the spirit himself bearing witness with our spirit that we are children of God.
Romans 8:15

Many years ago, I was asked to help plan a retreat for the clergy in my local geographical area. One of my tasks was to plan a communion service that would close the first day of the time together. The liturgy I selected had just recently been published. It was called the Lima Liturgy. This liturgy was the product of ecumenical dialogues among, Presbyterians, Lutherans, Roman Catholics, Anglicans, Methodists, Eastern Orthodox and several other Christian denominations. They sought to discuss their agreements and disagreements concerning Baptism, the Lord's Supper and Ordination.

The Liturgy produced by this meeting contains words that are agreed upon by almost all Christians around the world. It is a contemporary expression of ecumenical unity. I thought this would be a nice way of linking our Presbytery with the world church.

Boy was I wrong! Following this service, I was surrounded by at least four angry female ministers. They felt I had betrayed them and led a service that was hostile to women. It was not because of the preaching, for the person who gave the sermon was a woman. It was not because of anything I said off the cuff. It was the liturgy itself that raised the anger. This liturgy has a strong influence from the Eastern Orthodox Church which put a great emphasis on the Trinity. So again, and again throughout the Lima Liturgy there is a repetition of Father, Son and Holy Spirit.

In an age shaped by the feminist movement it is difficult for us to speak of God as Father. Now I believe that feminist theologians rightly criticize the Church for often only using male images of God.

It has been a positive corrective to be reminded that the Bible speaks of God using feminine imagery as well as male. God is said to be like a mother who comforts her children. This kind of picture of God has often been overlooked.

The female clergy who surrounded me that day suggested that we should seldom use the term Father in speaking of God. I disagree. In this chapter I would like to make three points about what it means when we call God, Father.

First, we should be clear that when we call God Father we are not declaring God is male. Many people grew up with a picture of God that includes a male figure sitting on a throne with a long white beard. Some people picture God as an austere figure with a severe judgmental look. There are others who see God as a kindly grandfather. These pictures are not all bad, but they should not be mistaken for reality.

These images may be helpful for some, but we need to remember that God does not have a gender. I think it is important to remind us that the image of God as Father does not imply a caring image for all people. There are many people for whom the term Father does not bring a warm image. The experience for many is that the term Father means a cold controlling presence or possibly a person who abused them or increasingly in our culture Father is someone who has abandoned them. Thus, to say that God is to be called Father can turn some people away from God.

Therefore, we need to balance our metaphors for God. Again, the women's movement over the last forty years has made a positive contribution in reminding us of the truth that God is neither male nor female. There are passages in the Bible that speak of God's nurturing love as being like a hen gathering her chicks under her wing. We need to use the full panorama of images, pictures and metaphors that include male and female.

God is not male or female. God is beyond gender. It was God who created gender. We read in the book of Genesis that "male and female God created them." Gender is a part of the created world; it is not part of the nature of God. Thus, when we refer to God as Father, we are not saying we believe God is male.

Secondly, we call God Father because we believe in a personal God. One of the differences between the eastern and western religions is the understanding of ultimate reality. The religions of the east such as Hinduism and Buddhism believe that God is an impersonal force. These faith systems do not profess belief in a personal God. The western understanding of the importance of the uniqueness of individuals is just an illusion for a Buddhist.

The goal of life for a Buddhist is to gain Nirvana. This means to end the cycle of reincarnation. Nirvana comes from a root word meaning, "blown out." The goal is for the individual to cease to exist and become part of the impersonal divine reality. This comes about by a process of increasing our understanding of the oneness of being. It means learning to give up our uniqueness as a human individual.

Nirvana indicates the gaining of the state of emptiness of craving and desire and giving up all those things that make us unique. This enables one to become one with the universe.

In contrast to eastern teaching, all the western religions believe that God is a personal God. Jews teach that Yahweh is one and separate from the created order. Islam calls each individual person to radical obedience to the one God

Jesus tells us in his prayer to call God, Father. In those words, we are taught to relate to the divine in a personal way. We join with Jews and Moslems in believing in a personal God. We are not to relate to an impersonal "ground of being ", but rather to seek a person to person encounter with God.

A third point follows for our belief in a personal God. While all western religions believe in a personal god, Jesus tells us that our primary interaction with God is based on love. We believe in a God who loves us and wants us to respond with love for him.

A young Roman Catholic girl came home from school one day and told her parents that their Irish priest was God. Her parents wondered how she came to that conclusion. They asked her questions seeking to ascertain the reasons for her deduction. Finally, the little girl reminded her parents that every week at Mass the whole congregation would stand and recite the creed. "We believe in one God, the Father O'Malley."

The young girl of course had gotten the creed wrong, but not as wrong as we might think. She was describing a basic truth that we believe in a personal God who cares for us. Every time we affirm the creed we say that we believe in a Father who loves us.

In Moslem cities around the world there are Mosques with towers called minarets. Five times a day the muezzin's climb the tower and call people to prayer with words beginning, "There is no God but God." A favorite phrase for Moslems is "God is great." The name Moslem means "one who submits."

These words reflect the relationship of a believer with God. The emphasis is on the oneness, greatness, and power of God. The duty of the believer is to submit to this great power. While God is personal, God is wholly other. God cannot be represented or depicted in this world. The believer can only bow in adoration and obedience to God.

In the Jewish faith God is unknowable, but his law can be obeyed. In the Book of Exodus Moses met God at the burning bush. He was told that he must go to Egypt to free the people. Moses asked a question of the voice. He wanted to know God's name. Moses asked, "Whom shall I say has sent me?" The voice responded with an obscure answer. The voice responded not with a noun but rather with the verb, "to be." It said, "Tell them I am has sent you."

This name indicated the complete otherness of God. The great I am is not part of this world. He is a wholly transcendent God. Men and women cannot name him nor can they represent him with pictures or anything fashioned from human hands. Indeed, the name Yahweh given to Moses was never to be pronounced by Jews. The name was so holy it could not be repeated.

Later, this same God gave Moses a great gift on Sinai. This gift was the commandments. The law was God's great gift to his people. Jews believed that the way people relate to the personal God is through obedience to his law. Almost all Jewish life can be understood as an attempt to follow Yahweh's laws in daily life.

The leaders of the Jewish people, who are called Rabbis, are in a very real sense lawyers. They are trained to help interpret God's law for people in daily life. As the reality of life changes, the rabbis seek to understand the law considering new realities. An example was when cars were invented the rabbis had to determine whether it was lawful to drive on the Sabbath.

In Islam, the faithful submit to the supreme power of Allah. In Judaism, the faith seeks to obey the law given by Yahweh.

In the first words of the Lord's Prayer, Jesus gave us a new name for God, a name that is to shape our relationship with him. Jesus called God, not Allah, not Yahweh, but Our Father. Jesus is teaching us that we too should name God as Father, a Father who cares for us.

There are examples in other religions of calling God Father, but they do so in a different way. Jesus is not speaking of God as Father in an abstract way. Indeed, the term Abba is more intimate than Father. It should be thought of as Daddy. We can call God Daddy. For Jesus, God is not reason or law or power, God is a living personality. This name of Father is to shape our relationship with God. There is a heart in God that loves us and wants us to respond with love. This is the fundamental nature of God on which Christianity is based.

Jesus tells us to call God Father because for him God is a loving caretaker of his people. The name Father does not erase the might, majesty and power of God. It does not make God anything less than God, but it does make the might and power approachable for us.

You and I can call God Father because Jesus has called us into relationship with him. Jesus our brother teaches us that God loves each one of us. Our picture of God is not primarily to be one that envisions God as judge, king or remoter creator. The central image is of God as a loving parent. Our approach to God is shaped by the name Father. Our primary offering to God is not obedience or submission but rather love. What God wants most from us is our hearts.

When we affirm God as Father we are not saying we believe in a male deity, rather we proclaim trust in a personal God who loves us.

Questions

>   1. What has been your primary mental image of God?
>   2. Does the word Father have positive or negative connotations for you?
>   3. What other images of God featuring the feminine are helpful to you?

Prayer

Loving God you came to us in Jesus to provide new ways for us to think of you? You are a nurturing God who cares for us as individuals. Give us new and fresh images that they might stir in us longing to be in relationship with you. Amen.

Chapter VI

The Maker

And God saw everything that he had made, and behold, it was very good.

Genesis 1:31

For all of its aura of mystery,
For all of its sense of the spiritual,
Christianity is a very worldly religion.

While our faith does give us a promise of heaven, the Christian understanding of creation points us towards this earth. One of my favorite phrases in the Nicene Creed is **We believe in one God the Father Almighty, Maker of heaven and earth, and of all things visible and invisible.** My very favorite words are all things visible and invisible or as another translation tells us of all that is, seen and unseen.

In this chapter, we explore what it means for us to call God the Maker of all things. In the first chapter of Genesis we are told the story of creation. God creates the universe out of nothing and then pronounces that all that has been created is good.

The Doctrine of Creation teaches us many important lessons. I would like us to focus on five important teachings we affirm when we call God the maker of all things.

First, it teaches us that the creation is not God. God is outside of the created order. Many primitive religions taught that God was in nature. There were often Gods of thunder or the sea or other elemental forces of nature. There was a tendency to worship nature.

In modern America, there has been a renewal of nature worship. In some of the radical wings of the environmental movement and in New Age religions there are people who identify God with nature. Some would try to teach us that when one hurts something in nature one hurts God. I want to be clear. Nature can point beyond itself to the creator, but nature is not part of God's self. God does not live in trees or lakes or mountains. When we destroy nature we sin against God, we do not injure God. I have heard stories of people who when cutting down a tree pray to the tree for forgiveness. God is the creator of tress, but he does not live in them. Thus, you and I are not to worship the created order, but rather respect it. The doctrine of creation reminds us of the distinction between God and God's creation.

Secondly when we say we believe in God the maker we affirm the goodness of the world.

There has been a tragic tendency in Christian history to over emphasize the spiritual nature of the faith. While it is correct to teach that God is wholly other, this should not lead to view the material world as being completely corrupt. There have been many Christian teachers who would appear to have taught that all that is wrong with the world could be traced to the fallenness of the material world and the passions of the flesh.

There has been a tendency in Christianity to believe in a dualism that sees the spiritual and material in opposition to each other. There are many who have viewed the spiritual as being all-good and the material as being the focus of evil.

Yet God pronounced all creation to be good. Furthermore, we learn that God became flesh in Jesus. God took on the earthiness of existence. Jesus had a body with all the regular functions. In becoming flesh, Jesus reaffirmed the goodness of creation. All our human passions are blessed by our creator. God takes delight in human joy experienced with our bodies.

This is illustrated in a great scene from the movie Chariots of Fire. This movie tells the story of Eric Liddell. Eric was a Scottish runner who won a gold medal at the Olympics in the 1920's. His sister felt that his athletic competition distracted him from his real calling which was to be a missionary in China. She believed that his running was not important to God. During a walk in the country outside of Edinburgh she attempted to convince him that a mere physical activity is of no importance. Eric's response was "When I run I feel

God's pleasure." Eric knew that God had given the physical world and pronounced it good.

The passage from Genesis goes further. The word in the Septuagint that is translated as good can also be translated at beautiful. Thus, God looked at the world he had created and said that it was beautiful. It would almost seem that the Sabbath found after this text is to be a time when we join God in pondering the beauty of his creation

Who would deny the sheer wonder and beauty of the created order? There are times we have experiences of beauty that overwhelm us. Artists can help us see this beauty. They produce in microcosm the real beauty of the universe and present it to others for contemplation. All of this affirms the point that creation is beautiful and good.

The fourth lesson for us is that we are not just asked to nod our heads in assent to the truth that creation is beautiful and has value. We are called to respond. All of nature is God's creation, but he has made us caretakers of creation. We demonstrate our love for God by caring for creation.

This begins by our loving nature. We nurture that love by experiencing creation. This means taking time to ponder the beauty and grandeur of the creation. It means teaching our children to respect nature. For people who live in cities this may mean visiting Zoos or Aquariums or farms. Hunting and fishing are positive experiences in part because they bring people into contact with the natural world.

Our love of nature will lead us to confess that we have failed to be good caretakers of our environment we, as a people, have been so preoccupied with creating wealth and using goods and services that we have not always been concerned with preserving and protecting nature.

One of the congregations I served was less than three miles from Love Canal. This ecological disaster was not done with a malicious intent. It was caused mostly by a complete lack of concern. Until the last forty years, Americans have lived with a headlong pursuit of wealth-without a concern for the effects on the natural world.

We each must confess to our Creator God that we have misused that which he has given us. When we confess that we have failed to protect his creation, grace forgives us and empowers us to change. Do not get me wrong; I am not saying we must cease to produce material goods. But we must produce them in a responsible manner.

The principle we should seek to follow is sustainability. This is the same rule that many churches set for groups using their buildings. There is usually one basic rule, "Please leave the building as you found it." Groups are often reminded if you break something replace it. They are expected to clean up their garbage and put the furniture back where they found it. If one group took all the tables and chairs with them or left garbage everywhere, then the next group would be unable to function in the space.

So, keeping the creation means that each generation must attempt to leave the creations at least as healthy as they found it.

The fifth lesson concerns our own personal stewardship. The most basic ethical teaching is that all that we have has been given to us in trust by a loving God.

When our granddaughter Emma turned one year old, she was beginning to say a few words like Daddy and Mommy and something that sounded like dog. In the coming year there is one word that I am sure she will learn. That word is mine. It is amazing how quickly two year olds want to claim everything around them as their property.

I am a great believer in our economic system. Our system of private property, the rule of law and relatively free markets has created more wealth and spread prosperity more broadly than any other economic system in history. In a recent book Arthur Brooks tells us that since 1980 "Billions of souls around the world have been able to pull themselves out of poverty thanks to five incredible innovations: globalization, free trade, property rights, the rule of law, and entrepreneurship."

The danger in all this success is that we will not grow beyond the two-year-old who says "Mine." We can believe that we have created what we have all on our own. We do not learn that all we have comes from God as a trust. Thus, a true meaning of stewardship is learning to use responsively what God has given us.

All too often the concept of stewardship is reduced to the church asking for money. This is uncomfortable for both the clergy and the congregation. It also ignores the truth that stewardship is a spiritual practice. We often act as if we believe that what we do with our material goods is our own business. We seldom see the connection between our use of our money and our relationship with God. You and I are called to grow spiritually through sharing our gifts.

Sharing our material gifts is a spiritual issue. This is probably the most difficult truth for many of us to accept. Jesus is concerned with how we use our financial resources. Let me be clear. Jesus does not require that we all live as monks forsaking all enjoyment of the material world. We are not called to be unconcerned about making money. There is nothing morally wrong with making a large income.

In addition, it is not wrong to enjoy the material benefits of our labor. The reality of the human condition is that we will use the greatest percentage of the gifts God has given us on our families and ourselves. We are to care for our families by providing, shelter, food, clothing and all the other necessities of life. It is not selfish or evil for us to fulfill our obligations to those closest to us.

Yet Jesus tells us that we grow through sharing our gifts.

A Christian is called to grow in giving to others as a way to give to God.

A story is told about a time a minister was giving a sermon on "total giving" When it came time to take up the offering, the plate came to a pew where there was a very small boy. He looked up at the usher and said, "Could you lower the plate?" Thinking that he wanted to see into the plate, the usher held it down a bit. "No," said the boy, "a little lower please." The usher lowered it a bit more. "More; could you just put it on the floor?" The boy asked. The usher was aghast but finally put it on the floor. The boy stepped into it, stood there, and said, "This is what I give to the Lord."

The boy has caught the idea that all that he has comes from God and he is to use it wisely.

When we affirm that God is the maker of all things this is not some abstract idea with little connection with everyday life. When we recognize that God is the source of all we have it calls us to be good caretakers and stewards of all we have received.

Questions

1. Do you perceive the material world as being unspiritual?
2. Do you understand the created order to be beautiful?
3. Do you accept that all you have belongs to God?
4. Have you broadened your view of Stewardship to include all of life?

Prayer

Creator God, we give you thanks for the wonder and beauty of the created order. We rejoice in the diversity in the created order. We have deep gratitude for water and air that we often take for granted. Help us to be good caretakers of all that you have given us. Teach us to take the stewardship of all our life to be a primary Christian calling. Amen,

Chapter VII

Fully God

Do you not believe that I am in the Father and the Father in me? These words I say to you I do not speak on my own authority; but the Father who dwells in me does his works. Believe me that I am in the Father and the Father in me.

John 14:10

The Gospels teach us that at one critical turning point in Jesus' earthly pilgrimage he asked his disciples, "Who do you say that I am?"

Who is Jesus is a question that has been the focus of discussion, controversy, and conflict for almost 2000 years. In the early centuries of the church Bishops lost their position because they gave controversial answers to this question. Churches have split over various responses to this question. Over the last twenty years we have experienced a myriad of controversies over the nature of Jesus. Remember how the popular novel "**The Da Vinci Code** accused the church of covering up Jesus' true identity. Mel Gibson's movie on the Passion of Jesus stirred up deep reactions pro and con in his violent portrayal of Jesus' last hours on the earth. The Jesus seminar, a group of professors, has sought to discover the "real" Jesus behind the New Testament text. Borg, Funk and others have presented their personal understanding of who Jesus is.

In this chapter, we move to the second article of the Creed which deals with the person and work of the Son. The early councils of the Church answered the question of Jesus' identity by stating a paradox. They claimed that Jesus was both fully God and fully human. In these next two chapters, we focus on each side of this paradox.

When we read the Gospels the disciples, time and time again, just do not seem to get it. At the end of his earthly ministry, we find Jesus in the Upper Room. This is his last night on earth before his death. He spends this time with his closest companions. These are his followers; most of them have been with him for three years. They have witnessed everything he has done. They have heard him teach. They knew him better than anyone on earth.

Philip asked Jesus a question. He asked Jesus to show us the Father. The questions seemed to frustrate Jesus. Philip clearly still does not know Jesus' true identity. Jesus replied, **"Have I been with you so long and yet you do not know me Philip? He who has seen me has seen the Father; how can you say show us the Father?"**

Then in the words that follow Jesus clearly identifies himself with God the Father.

Do you not believe that I am in the Father and the Father in me? These words I say to you I do not speak on my own authority; but the Father who dwells in me does his works. Believe me that I am in the Father and the Father in me.

Philip is chastised for not knowing that Jesus is God. Yet throughout the New Testament people seemed to always get it wrong.

There were some who thought of Jesus as a military leader. Many of the people who were attracted to Jesus believed he was the Messiah who would lead the people of Israel to victory over the Romans. The Romans had captured Palestine. A Roman governor set policy. There many people who believed that Jesus was the long-promised redeemer who could set the people free. They expected that Jesus would arm the crowds and form an army.

There were others of Jesus' day who thought him a teacher. They called him Rabbi. They believed he was a sincere good teacher who brought God's message in a clear way.

These and other understandings of Jesus pictured him as merely a human being. Yes, a special man, yes, an important man, yes, a unique person, but still only a person of flesh and blood like us.

Even as the first followers of Jesus died off, the church continued to wrestle with the question-who is Jesus? There were many disagreements as to the nature of Jesus in the first centuries after the resurrection. Again, there some who conceived of Jesus as being a good role model, a perfect teacher or a flawless human. But they all seemed to agree that in his life, death and resurrection somehow, they experienced salvation.

The discussion became very heated in the fourth century when some leaders of the Church began to deny that Jesus was fully God. The conflict became so severe that it threatened the unity of the Church. Constantine who was the Roman Emperor became worried that this internal church conflict might spill over and threaten the unity of his empire. He encouraged the leaders of the Church to gather at Nicea to settle the question.

Leaders from around the world gathered at Nicea and after a season of prayer, arguments, conflict and more prayer they formulated an answer that shapes our understanding until today. They understood that Jesus was fully God. In the creed, they declared:

We believe in one Lord, Jesus Christ, the only Son of God, eternally begotten of the Father, God from God, Light from Light, true God from true God, begotten not made, being of one substance with the Father.

The writers of this creed pound home the point that Jesus is fully God through repetition: God from God, Light from Light, true God from true God.

The creed states that Jesus is of one substance or one being with the Father, which is to say he is fully God. He participates fully in the Godhead. The followers of Jesus in those early centuries knew that somehow, they were saved by Jesus' life, death and resurrection. They also knew only God could save. Therefore, to deny that Jesus was fully God was to deny the reality of salvation through Jesus. The leaders at Nicea were determined that all should be reminded that God came to us in Jesus to offer forgiveness and the hope of eternal life.

Now it is all well and good to say that the church settled the question in the early fourth century. This still does not excuse each one of us from answering the question for ourselves. Each one of us must decide for ourselves who we believe Jesus really is.

In one of his most famous passages in Mere Christianity, C.S. Lewis claimed that we have three basic choices concerning the nature of Jesus. After talking about many of the things that Jesus said and did, such as forgiving sins, he writes:

> **I am trying here to prevent anyone saying the really foolish thing that people often say about Him: 'I'm ready to accept Jesus as a great moral teacher, but I don't accept His claim to be God.' That is the one thing we must not say. A man who was merely a man and said the sort of things Jesus said would not be a great moral teacher. He would either be a lunatic — on a level with the man who says he is a poached egg — or else he would be the Devil of Hell. You must make your choice. Either this man was, and is, the Son of God or else a madman or something worse. You can shut Him up for a fool, you can spit at Him and kill Him as a demon; or you can fall at His feet and call Him Lord and God. But let us not come with any patronizing nonsense about His being a great human teacher. He has not left that open to us. He did not intend to."**

Each one of us must make a choice. Was Jesus a person with a delusional messiah complex? Was he an evil man who attempted to manipulate people by claiming to be divine? Or was he exactly who he claimed to be, God himself?

Some of you may say wait a minute, why are these the only choices. There are many who have thought that Jesus is primarily a teacher. Many modern writers have claimed that we should understand Jesus as a moral reformer like Moses or Mohammed. The members of the Jesus Seminar wanted to portray Jesus as a good man. They have said that there are limited passages in which Jesus directly claims his Sonship. Could not the writers of the Gospels have heard incorrectly?

The problem with this position is that the reality of Jesus claiming his oneness with God is found not only in isolated passages. Jesus' actions throughout the Gospels betray his unity with God.

Think of how many times Jesus takes God's authority upon himself. The Jewish people of the first century believed that God had spoken to his people most clearly in the first five books of the Old Testament which they call the law, the Torah. The task of teachers was to understand and interpret God's law for the present day. The scribes and Pharisees were in effect lawyers who spent hours studying the meaning of God's law.

Then Jesus came along and began to reshape the law. Time and again in the Gospels we hear Jesus say, "You have heard it said of old that.... But I say to you..." Jesus gave not just a new interpretation but new meaning. He spoke on his own authority. He took unto himself the authority reserved for God.

If I went into the pulpit one Sunday morning and read a passage from the Sermon on the Mount which tells us to love our enemies, and I then said, "You know this passage is only Jesus' opinion, but I say to you it is better to hit back at your enemy before they get a chance to respond." I am sure that the people present would be upset and I hope they would be. They would wonder who Greg thinks he is to place himself above the words of Jesus. Many might ponder, "Who does he think he is, God?"

Yet this is exactly what Jesus did. He spoke with his own authority. He took on the role of God.

Even more shocking in the Gospels is the way that Jesus forgives people their sins. We are so used to the idea that Jesus forgives our sins that we are unaware of the shocking nature of Jesus' words. Time and again people come to Jesus to hear his teaching or for healing and Jesus tells then, "Go, your sins are forgiven."

Suppose for a moment your neighbor one night set your house on fire. Your house burns to the ground and everyone is killed in the house but you. In the morning if I showed up in the neighborhood and your neighbor says, "I feel terrible." If I said, "It is all right your sins are forgiven" I am sure you would be furious or at least confused. What right would I have to forgive someone a wrong they committed against you?

Yet Jesus went around forgiving sins all the time. This is something only God can do. When Jesus was charged with blasphemy this was part of the reason. He took on himself the prerogatives of God. Throughout the Gospels Jesus speaks and acts in ways that identify him with God. His words and deeds are summed up in his words: **Believe me that I am in the Father and the Father in me.**

Several years ago, PBS aired a special on the tragedy at Waco, Texas. If you remember, early in the Clinton Administration a small religious sect called the "Branch Davidians" had shot some federal officers when they tried to serve a warrant. The FBI and other government authorities surrounded the compound. This PBS special traced step by step the decision-making process of the Justice Department that eventually led to the tear gas assault and fire that took the lives of many men, women and children. Much of the program centered on the government negotiator as they tried to bring a peaceful conclusion to the standoff.

At one point in the program, the lead negotiator for the government reported that they had to make a decision about David Koresh. Koresh was the leader of the Branch Davidians. He talked about himself being the messiah. He held absolute control of his followers. The government negotiators had to decide whether Koresh was a delusional crazy who truly believed he was the messiah, or was he a con-man who used his teaching to manipulate his followers. The answer to this question would determine their response to him.

The central question of the Christian faith is, "Who is this Jesus?" Our answer will determine how we respond to him.

Was Jesus mentally ill, having delusions of grandeur?
Was he a charlatan who manipulated his followers?
Was he merely a good teacher?
Or is he the eternal Son of God made flesh?

I believe that Jesus is a miracle of God.
I believe that the divine came to earth in Jesus.
When I want to know who God is I picture Jesus.
When I want to know what God wants of me, I listen to Jesus.

When I desire forgiveness I ask Jesus,
For Jesus is the fullness of God made manifest in the world

Who do you say Jesus is?

Questions to ponder

> 1. How many names do you use for Jesus?
> 2. Do you think of Jesus primarily in his human role or his divine role?
> 3. What one sentence would you use to describe who Jesus is?

Prayer

Saving God, you have come to us in Jesus to reveal your nature to us. As we study the earthly life of your Son, may we discover the love that you have for us. Give us the ability to affirm the fullness of your divinity in Jesus. Amen.

Chapter VIII

Fully Human

Because He himself has suffered and been tempted, he is able to help those who are tempted.
Hebrews 2:18

I left the church because it no longer seemed relevant to my problems.
I had already been saved
And I was looking for some help living in this world,
Before it was time to go to heaven

In college, my fragile faith bit the dust.

Working on a truck line loading freight crushed the vision of Camelot.

These fragments from a young man's autobiography reveal what many of us can feel at different times in our life. During our everyday struggles, we may sense an absence of God. We can wonder what Jesus has to do with my regular daily routine. We can question how does a figure from the first century relate to our struggles today? What can the divine Christ who is fully God know about so called real life?

In this chapter, we come to the words **For us and for our salvation he came down from heaven, was incarnate of the Holy Spirit and the Virgin Mary and became truly human.** These words remind us of the second part of the paradox that we began to explore in the previous chapter. We focused on the truth that Jesus was fully God; today we ponder the truth that Jesus was fully human.

One of the bestselling novels of the last twenty years, which was also made into a movie starring Tom Hanks, was *The Da Vinci Code*. In this very entertaining book Dan Brown made the accusation that the early church conspired to cover up the humanity of Jesus. He tells us that the Church made up the myth of Jesus being fully God and ignored his humanity.

This argument is anachronistic. While the modern mentality can make it difficult for people today to conceive of how Jesus could be divine, it was the reverse in the first several centuries of Christian History. In the years following Jesus' resurrection many groups of Christians found it hard to believe that Jesus had been fully human. The Church had to continually fight to maintain that Jesus was a human person who existed in an earthly body. Men and women who were attracted to the Christian movement wanted to turn Jesus into a purely spiritual being. There were many who denied Jesus really had a body.

We see this tension present in the Gospels. In the prologue of his Gospel, John writes about the eternal word of God who has been present since before creation. The first verses celebrate the divine and spiritual nature of the word. But then John takes a sharp turn and culminates in the affirmation that declares Jesus was fully human-**and the word became flesh and dwelt among us.**

The words **and the word became flesh** remind us that the creed tells us **he came down from heaven, was incarnate of the Holy Spirit and the Virgin Mary and became truly human.** Jesus lived a fully normal human existence. It was to a young Jewish peasant girl name Mary that Jesus was born. He came into the world as we all do, to the accompaniment of cries of physical pain and inward spiritual joy. As William Blake put it:

**My mother groaned, my father wept.
Into the dangerous world I leapt.**

Jesus was born in a stable or outbuilding, a cave maybe, since no other more suitable accommodation was available within the means of Mary and Joseph. He began life as part of a humble human family.

We believe that Jesus lived a full human life. The Bible teaches us that Jesus experienced life in all its many faceted dimensions. Jesus was not some kind of superman who walked above the difficulties of life with bullets bouncing off his body. Jesus did not just play act a human life.

There may be times we picture Jesus as being part human and part divine. This is what I call the invasion of the body snatchers view of Jesus. In this image God takes over a human body. In this formulation Jesus is made up of two parts. He would have had a human part that consists of a natural body. But the rest of Jesus, his personality, will and mind is divine. In this view Jesus is sort of like a Jack 'o' lantern. The human inside is hollowed out and filled with the light of God's presence. Jesus is half man and half God.

One of the great paradoxes of our faith is our proclamation that Jesus was both fully human and fully divine. Just as we will never fully comprehend the truth that God is three persons in one nature in the Trinity, so we cannot fully grasp that in the one person, Jesus, there are two natures. While Jesus was fully God, we also teach he was fully human.

He had a human body.
He had a human will.
He had a human mind
He had human emotions.
He experienced human temptations.

In short, Jesus lived a full human life.

This difficult teaching is not just some abstract theological concept. It is not just something that interests theologians who also like to number the angels dancing on the head of a pin. The full humanity of Christ teaches us that God understands our lives. Jesus knows what human life is like and thus can stand with us in every experience of our lives.

The writer of Hebrews tells us: **Because He himself has suffered and been tempted, he is able to help those who are tempted.** Because Jesus has experienced every aspect of life-he understands us.

If you are a child in school working hard to learn how to read and write-If you are worried about an upcoming test-Jesus understands for he spent time learning from the Rabbi how to read the Torah.

You may be a teenager who is struggling to find your identity independent of your parents. You may be going through a time where one minute you love your parents and the next minute you are furious with them. Jesus understands for he too staked out his independence from Mary and Joseph on a trip to Jerusalem when he was a teenager. He understands the turmoil of your emotions.

Each one of us faces temptations day in and day out. We all are faced with situations in our lives when we feel drawn to do something we know is wrong, whether cheating on a test, taking something which is not ours, telling a lie about someone, fudging on our taxes or something else. We all have felt how powerful temptation to violate our principles can be.

Jesus understands. In the wilderness Jesus underwent temptation to follow a different path which could have led to material success, political power or public acclaim. Jesus understands and will stand with us in our temptation.

In our lives, we undergo many experiences of loss. Each one of us at some time has faced the death of a loved one. We may lose our grandparent, parents, spouse, children or close friends. We face the trial of living our days without someone whom we love. We know the empty space in our hearts. Mourning is a profoundly difficult human experience.

Jesus experienced loss. We know that somewhere between the age of twelve and thirty, Joseph died. The Father who gave support, guidance and stability to Jesus' life was taken from him. Jesus knew the wound to his heart of mourning one who was loved.

When we mourn, Jesus cries with us for he understands our pain.

It is not only the difficult aspects of life that Jesus shares with us. He knew the joys of life as well. Jesus would have worked long hours in Joseph's shop. After the long day of physical toil, Jesus would have had the wonderful sense of peace when putting up his feet and relaxing after a nice meal.

Jesus was not some Victorian prude who stood off from the joys of life. Remember how Jesus went to a wedding feast in Cana. A celebration at which he acted to make sure the refreshments did not run out prematurely.

When we experience joy and happiness in life-Jesus celebrates with us.

When we struggle with moral dilemmas in life, Jesus stands with us. Each one of us has competing demands made on our time and energy. We can be torn between commitments to parents, spouses, children, jobs and friends.

Jesus knows this struggle. We can only guess at what happened during the middle years of Jesus' life. He may have begun to feel God's call on his life, yet Joseph had died and Jesus' had to take responsibility for his family. His earthly work may have been delayed until others in the family were old enough to take on responsibility.

So, when we seek to juggle our commitments, Jesus understands.

When we question the will of God,
when we wonder why something has happened to us,
when we are unsure of God's love for us,
Jesus knows how we feel.

Remember Jesus' experience in the Garden. It became clear to him that following God's will would mean his own death. Jesus was fully human; he did not want to die. In the Garden, he wrestled with God's purpose in his life. He may not have fully understood why, why did he have to die. Then on the cross Jesus goes further and wonders why God had forsaken him.

When we struggle with meaning in our lives, when we question God, Jesus is with us.

Finally, when we face our death, we are not alone. Jesus met his death on the cross. He has walked through the valley of death before us. Jesus knew the fear, pain and questions of facing the final journey of life. He has been there and Jesus will be with us when we make that final journey.

We believe that Jesus is fully human as well as fully God.

We believe in a God who understands us.
We trust a God who knows the good and bad of the human condition.
We love a Jesus who has shared our life and promises to be with us as we complete our journey.

Questions to ponder

>   1. Have you ever reflected on Jesus' human experiences?
>   2. Where are you today in your earthly pilgrimage?
>   3. How can Jesus support you in your life today?

Prayer

Loving Jesus, you know what life in the world is like. You have known joy and sorrow. You have known grief and loss and also celebrated weddings and healings. Help us to turn to you each day of our lives that we might know support and encouragement that only you can give. Amen.

Chapter IX

Suffered for Us

But He was wounded for our transgression, He was bruised for our iniquities; upon Him was the chastisement that makes us whole and with His stripes we are healed.

Isaiah 53:5

During World War II a Marine division was being briefed regarding a landing on one of the islands in the South Pacific. They were told. "Our artillery has been unable to dislodge the Japanese. When the first wave hits the beach probably only five out of a hundred will survive." One Marine private responded, "Gee I'm gonna miss all you guys."

Almost all of us are a little like that private. We find it hard to face difficult truths. Denial is a handy psychological tool for avoiding painful realities. In this chapter, we face some painful truths **For our sake he was crucified under Pontius Pilate; he suffered death and was buried.** Some might ask why the creed is so repetitious here. If he was crucified, he was obviously dead; and if he was dead, he would surely be buried. The Creed emphasizes what happened by saying it in three different ways-dead, dead, dead, like the tolling of a bell.

We often recite these words quickly and with little feeling. Yes, we acknowledge with our heads that Jesus died for us. Yes, we intellectually understand he had to die for our sins. But we run through these words so quickly that we do not have to focus on the reality of what truly happened to Jesus. We know that if we focus on these words too closely we may not be able to deal with them.

Sometimes even when we read the account of Jesus' Passion during Lent we tend to ignore the harsh reality of what happened. We quickly run to admire the forgiving words of Jesus **Father forgive them for they know not what they do.** Or we move our focus from Jesus' great promise to one of the criminals dying with him **I say to you today you will be with me in Paradise.**

The Nicene Creed's repetition of this hard reality reminds us of the great truth that **He was wounded for our transgression, He was bruised for our iniquities; upon Him was the chastisement that makes us whole and with His stripes we are healed.** I would like to focus on the reality which stands behind the words, **For our sake he was crucified under Pontius Pilate; he suffered death and was buried.** These are not abstract words, but rather an historical reality.

He was wounded for our transgressions.... Jesus in his love for us suffered the physical pain of crucifixion. Crucifixion was a form of punishment that was reserved for rebels, runaway slaves and common criminals. Jesus was condemned by Pilate and handed over to Roman executioners. The soldiers made sport with him. Jesus was beaten and scourged. Scourging meant that Jesus was beaten on the back with whips. The Romans used a leather whip. These whips were made more painful by pieces of lead or brass or small pieces of bone that were attached to the lashes so that they bit into the skin. The victim was stripped to the waist and attached to a pillar. The suffering was intense, the body was frightfully lacerated.

After undergoing the scourging, Jesus was handed the cross beam of the cross which weighed about 90 pounds. He was forced to carry it through the hot sun out of the city towards Calvary. When his strength failed a man named Simon was compelled by the soldiers to carry the cross while others helped Jesus along.

When they arrived at Golgotha, nails were driven through Jesus' wrists and ankles in order to attach him to the cross. He was then lifted into the air. Exposure to the elements, loss of blood, impaired circulation, hunger and difficulty breathing all contributed to the pain. Finally, after hours of pain it was over and Jesus was dead.

Jesus' love for us was so great that he endured the pain of scourging and crucifixion.

How can we refuse such a love?

But the physical pain and torture was not all that Jesus suffered. He was also afflicted with the total loss of his position and station in life. This kind of loss of personhood is experienced in our age by refugees all over the world. We can see it in the people of the Middle East. Men, women and children have been forced to flee by war or persecution. They live in permanent make shift camps. Many are trying to make their way to Europe. They have little shelter, not enough food and medical care is in short supply. They have been uprooted from their homes. They no longer have property, or homes or a position in society. In many ways, they have become non-persons.

Jesus on the cross was stripped of his personhood. As the Son of God, Jesus was one with the Father. He was a part of the creation of the world, yet on Calvary this seems to have been completely lost. He appears to be at the mercy of creation. All one can perceive is the powerlessness of a broken man. He is taunted by the Roman Soldiers **How can he save others, he cannot save himself.** Jesus on the cross has his personhood taken away. His identity is taken from him and he is treated as a common criminal. In the eyes of the people, Jesus is nothing. What often happens in this kind of affliction is that the victim begins to believe that they are worthless. The victim begins to agree that they are a non-person.

Because of his love for us, Jesus endured affliction.

How can we refuse this love?

On the cross Jesus suffered complete isolation from humanity. When someone is executed today in this country there are all kinds of people concerned with the person who is to be killed. There are wives and children and parents and friends and lawyers who are concerned. There are people who are supportive right to the end.

But Jesus in a very real sense was alone. All of his disciples had deserted him. Jesus had lived with them for over two years. They had shared his table. They had prayed with him, laughed with him, cried with him. The disciples had seen him heal people, they had heard him preach, they had been his friends, and surely, they would stick by him to the end. Yet in the pinch they fled. When we read the story in the synoptic Gospels we do not see any familiar faces in the crowd at the cross. Jesus is alone. In the Gospel of John, we do find a few women and John way off to the side. But really Jesus is left alone. The men who were around him nail him to the cross and then gamble for his clothes and taunt him.

Jesus in his pain suffers ultimate human rejection. The pain is more acute when we remember that it was for the very people who betrayed him, it was for the very people who ran away, and it was for the very people who nailed him to the cross that he died.

How can we refuse a love such as this?

Perhaps the greatest pain that Jesus endured on the cross, greater than the physical pain, greater than the loss of personhood, greater than the loss of human love, was the sense of complete isolation from God. Jesus came to the point where he cried out **My God, My God why hast Thou forsaken me?**

Jesus seemed to feel that God had abandoned him. He must have wondered what all this suffering was for. All have rejected him, why should he have to suffer this cruel torture? He knew that he had followed God's will all his life. He must have wondered why this would have led to a cross. What was the point or purpose for all the pain?

Yes, Jesus on that first Good Friday suffered complete isolation from God. Paul tells us that for our sakes he became sin. Jesus took our sins and the sins of the whole world upon himself. On that Jerusalem hillside, Jesus became sin itself dying on the cross. In a sense Jesus was further from the Father's love on that day than anything or anyone else in all creation has ever been.

He who had full and perfect communion with the Father came to be completely isolated from the Father's love. His death was in a very real sense the wrenching apart of God himself.

Because of his love for us, Jesus suffered the complete absence of the Father's love.

How can we refuse such a love as this?

One of the lines of poetry that has shaped my thinking comes from George Herbert's **The Temple.** In his poem that is a meditation on the sacrifice of Jesus on the cross, he has Jesus tell us one purpose of the cross in these words:

**I answer nothing, but with patience prove
If stony hearts will melt with gentle love.**

Herbert reminds us that in going to the cross, Jesus seeks to win us to his love. It is Jesus' humble sacrifice on the cross that calls us home.

When we remember the kind of love that Jesus showed for us on the cross, when we remember what happened to him. When we look with our mind's eye at the picture of Jesus with tears in his eyes hanging there suffering for us, we who know even a little about real love are drawn to his overpowering love. For the cross is the true picture of what love is all about.

If we allow ourselves to stand before the cross for even a moment we will discover if our stony hearts will melt from his gentle love. **For our sake, he was crucified under Pontius Pilate.**

How can you refuse a love such as this?

Questions to ponder

> 1. Have you ever used your imagination to ponder the depth of Jesus' suffering?
> 2. Have you experienced feeling abandoned by God?
> 3. Does Jesus' sacrifice move your heart to melt?

Prayer

Lord Jesus, we remember that you are the Lamb of God who takest away the sin of the world. That sacrifice is almost too overwhelming for us to fathom. Help us to sit at the foot of the cross and not be overcome by the gore and pain, but rather to wonder at the beauty of your love for us. Amen.

Chapter X

Christ is Alive!

I know that my redeemer lives, and at the last day he will stand upon the earth; and after my skin has been thus destroyed then from my flesh I shall see God.

Job 19:25

In this chapter, we move to a part of the Creed that gives us joy. In the previous chapters, we have seen a downward spiral of increasing gloom. Jesus was born, suffered, died and was buried. He experienced the complete absence of the Father. Now we experience a transition. We proclaim on the third day he rose again in accordance with the Scriptures.

This great transition is portrayed in the B-minor Mass by Bach. In the section of the Mass called Credo-the section with the words he was buried-ends with the wailing of strings, softer and softer until the sound dies away in despair. There is a moment of utter silence so heavy it weighs you down. Then the conductor raises the baton, and all the timpani and all the trumpets and all the singers burst forth with and "he rose again."

The joy of our faith comes from the bold claim that the same Jesus who suffered under Pontius Pilate, who was crucified, dead and buried, is now alive. Death could not hold him. He lives and is with us today.

In the Courtauld Gallery in London hangs a painting called "The Incredulity of St. Thomas" by Michelangelo. The painting depicts the scene in the upper room when the Risen Christ appeared to his disciples. Thomas, who is known as the doubter, is stretching out his hand to touch the wound in Christ's side. He cannot believe Jesus is alive again.

We too have difficulty accepting the great affirmation of our creed that Jesus arose from the dead. You and I live in an age of doubt in matters of faith, politics and morals. Agnosticism is our most comfortable mode of exposing ourselves to the world. We answer so many questions in tentative terms. We find it easy to couch our answers in phrases such as: It is only my opinion, or I think, or I hope, or I believe. There are times when our patterns of speech reveal that we are not sure we know anything.

It can be bracing for us when we come across an affirmation such as we find in Job, when he can boldly proclaim, "I know that my redeemer lives." We are surprised by the assurance of the disciples who preached "Christ is risen!" We want to have that same certainty. We have so many questions, "How can we know he is alive? How can we be sure? Can we proclaim with confidence that we believe Christ is Alive?"

I believe that if we focus on the experience of Mary Magdalene we can learn how she became convinced of the truth that Jesus had been raised.

When Mary Magdalene first met Jesus, she was at the end of her rope. Tradition teaches us that she was a prostitute. We do not know if this is true but whatever her situation she found herself on the margins of society and her life was in shambles. But Jesus' love had transformed her. His care had given her life meaning and purpose. She responded to his care and love.

But then she saw Jesus travel to Jerusalem. Before she barely knew what was happening Jesus was arrested. He was taken before Pilate and condemned to death. Mary was there at the fringes of the crowd as Jesus was nailed to the cross. All of Mary's hopes and dreams slipped away as Jesus' life ebbed away on the cross. The Sabbath was fast approaching and thus a proper burial could not be completed that Friday.

Mary was devastated. She was just beginning the process of mourning the loss of Jesus that first Easter morning. She arose early in the morning to get to the tomb. She had loved Jesus. He had transformed her life. She felt that she could perform one last act of respect and love. She could prepare his body for burial.

When she arrived at the tomb she found that it was empty. The body of Jesus was nowhere to be found. Mary sat down and began to cry. Her first reaction was to think that someone had stolen Jesus' body.

One of those who had hated Jesus must have come and committed one final act of cruelty by taking his body. The empty tomb did not give Mary a belief in the resurrection.

The empty tomb will not give us faith either. There are so many possible explanations for the body not being in the tomb. If we use our power of reason to explain the empty tomb, resurrection would not be our first answer. Our modern application of the scientific method cannot help us prove the resurrection. Science studies the way nature operates. It means performing experiments to see how the natural world works. The resurrection is not claimed to be a natural occurrence. It is a unique event. Paul claimed it was the first fruit. It only happened once in history, thus it is beyond the scope of science to give us assurance in the resurrection. The tomb was empty, but no matter how long we ponder it, it will not give us faith.

Mary was sitting by the empty tomb weeping, when someone came up to her and she asked what had happened to Jesus' body. Her weeping blinded her to the identity of the person. Then Jesus said, "Mary, Mary" and she recognized the Risen Christ. She then went to the disciples and told them that she has seen the Lord. It was the presence of the Risen Christ that gave her faith in his victory over death.

And so, it began. The Risen Christ appeared to those who loved him and mourned his death.

Please notice that the Risen Jesus does not try to force people to have faith in Him. The Risen Christ did not appear in Pilate's bedroom to say, "Here I am, I am the truth who you condemned." The Risen Lord did not reveal himself to the Jewish authorities. He could well have come before the San Hedrin and made them believe that his way of interpreting the Jewish Scriptures was correct. He did not appear to the Roman Soldiers. He did not go to the Praetorium and say. "Here are the hands you nailed to the cross; here is the side you pierced with a spear." He did not appear before the mob in the square in front of the temple in Jerusalem and call them to faith. The Risen Christ did not appear to those who rejected the earthly Jesus.

And today, the Risen Christ is not going to appear on the Today Show, Bill O'Reilly or Oprah to answer questions in order to convince skeptics.

God does not want to use force to make people believe in Him. Jesus in his earthly life sought to win men and women by love. He did not use divine power to coerce people into obeying him. He sought to demonstrate such a love for us that we would love him. Jesus wants our love, not our fear.

It is interesting to study the appearances of the Risen Christ in the Gospels. He appeared only to those who had loved him and mourned his death. First, he appeared to Mary then Peter and John and many others. Thomas could not believe that Jesus was really alive when others told him. He responded with contempt for the message, yet he too had loved Jesus and the Risen Christ came to him and he believed. Down through the ages countless men and women who love the picture of Jesus presented in the Gospels have come to know the presence of the Risen Lord.

Jesus continues to reveal his presence to this very day.

In the early 1990's, Isvestia the old Soviet News Service carried this quote from Boris Yelstin which convinced me that the old atheistic Soviet system was finished. Yeltsin said:

> **I will speak for myself. First of all, I am baptized. My name and date of birth, as was the rule, was written in the baptismal registry. My grandparents were believers, as were my father and mother, until we left the country for the city. Later, in the course of a disproportionately ideological formation at school and in university, I constantly heard read, -and why hide it- felt and shared the most insulting opinions concerning the Church and religion. The education was gravely wrong and seriously unjust, as was the classification of persons into believers and no-believers, a distinction which today is somewhat blurred. Having said this, I have the greatest respect for the Orthodox Church, for its history, for its contribution to Russian spiritual life, for its moral teachings, its**

tradition of mercy and charity. Today the church is moving ahead in these areas, and our duty to it, is in turn to reestablish the rights of the Church. When I am in a Church I take a candle. A religious service lasting four hours bores neither me nor my wife. And often, when I leave a church, I feel that something new, something luminous, has come into me.

The luminous presence is the Risen Christ.

What about you and me? If we approach the idea of resurrection with only a casual interest, if we are only concerned with our own personal destiny. If we only come to see if the tomb is empty so that we can have a little hope that death will not be the end for us, then the claims of Christianity will mean little to us. At best, it will give us a little assurance.

But if we mourn the death of Jesus, if we realize that Jesus died on the Cross because of us, if we are sorry that he had to die for our sins then the resurrection is only a beginning. When we come in love, the Risen Christ makes his presence known to us. He will be with us for all eternity.

Whenever we come to the Lords' table we celebrate Jesus' victory over death. We open the deepest parts of our souls to receive again the presence of the Risen Christ into our hearts

If we love the sacrifice of the earthly Jesus,
If we give our hearts to the Jesus of the Gospels,
The Risen Christ will make his presence known to us.

Questions to ponder

> 1. What makes the concept of the resurrection hard to believe?
> 2. Do you relate to Mary's experience?
> 3. Have you ever known "a luminous experience?

Prayer

Risen Lord, so often it is hard for us to fathom the reality of the resurrection. Help us to focus our minds and hearts on the love of Jesus found in the Gospels. May we mourn your death and so be open to your coming to us. Amen.

Chapter XI

The Cosmic Christ

Jesus said, "Lo, I am with you always, even to the end of the age."

John 5:22

In this chapter, we focus on some of the strangest words in the creed **he ascended into heaven.**

The Ascension of Jesus can often conjure up some strange images in our minds. Some of these pictures can make the event seem surreal. As a child of the sixties, there are times when I read this account in Luke or Acts that I can almost hear the music from the Fifth Edition:

Up, Up and away in my beautiful balloon, my beautiful balloon.

This makes the event into some kind of joy ride. The ascension would seem almost a ludicrous happening.

I grew up in the days before VCR's, DVD's and Netflix. We did not have the ability to see any movie on demand. Every year we would look forward to the annual showing of the movie **The Wizard of Oz** on television. For many children, this was one of the most important Sunday nights of the year. This movie is filled with the adventures of Dorothy, the girl from Kansas in the magical Land of Oz. You may remember that at the end of the movie, Dorothy is to be taken back to Kansas by the Wizard in a hot air balloon. Just as they are about to lift off, Dorothy's dog Toto runs after a cat and Dorothy runs off to retrieve him. The ropes holding the balloon are untied and the Wizard slowly drifts off into the sky leaving Dorothy and Toto behind. She is left on the ground calling for him to come back and not leave her behind without hope of seeing Kansas again.

The picture of Dorothy looking up as the Wizard leaves her behind is one of abandonment. It can fill us with sadness and a sense of loss.

Often, I have read the story of Jesus' Ascension with the scene from the Wizard of Oz in my mind. I can almost see Jesus slowly going up towards the heavens leaving his disciples behind to fend for themselves.

The Ascension of Jesus might seem like he was leaving his disciples all alone. We might think of this event as indicating that God has abandoned the world. We might believe that he no longer cares for his creation and that he cannot be found here in this life. It must have been, we would think, a time of great sadness for Jesus' followers. The Risen Lord was no longer with them in the body.

Yet surprisingly there is no sadness found in the Bible. The record of the Ascension is found in Luke and the Book of Acts. In neither book is there a mood of despair. Indeed, in Luke we are told that after Jesus had ascended the disciples returned to Jerusalem with great joy.

They experienced this joy because they knew that the limits of the incarnation had been broken. Jesus had taken on the limits of time and space in becoming a human being subject to the laws of nature. In returning to the Father, the constraints of being in the flesh were now broken. The Risen Christ could now be present across time and space. The disciples were joyful for now they could experience the Risen Christ even more fully. He had promised to be with them even to the end of the age. In his Ascension Jesus becomes the Cosmic Christ.

You and I might ask where is God?
Where is Christ at work?
How do I know God is present?

The Risen Christ is present in history. The testimony of the Scriptures is that God is at work in history. The Bible itself is the record of God's interaction with his people. It records his saving purpose in the lives of humankind.

Of course, it is not always obvious to us in the midst of history. Yet the same God who delivered the people of Israel from slavery in

Egypt, the same God who allowed the people of Judah to be defeated and carried into exile is at work today.

George Bancroft was one of the great 19th century American historians. He lived through the carnage of the Civil War. In one of his books he asks this question:

> **Do nations float darkly alone down the stream of the ages without hope or consolation, swaying with every wind, and ignorant whither they are drifting? Or is there a Superior Power of intelligence and love, which is moved by justice and shapes their forces?**

The Bible has a plain answer to that question, for it tells us that God is the Supreme Actor in history, and that great men and women and great nations and movements are but the brief embodiment and transient realization of his desires. Often in the midst of history we try to get God on our side instead of trying to find where God might be at work.

President Lincoln wrestled with these questions in his second inaugural address:

> **Both read the same Bible and pray to the same God, and each invokes His aid against the other. It may seem strange that any men should dare to ask a just God's assistance in wringing their bread from the sweat of other men's faces, but let us judge not, that we be not judged. The prayers of both could not be answered. That of neither has been answered fully. The Almighty has His own purposes.**

Even though we live in a time when the world seems to be coming apart at the seams- a time when nothing seems to make sense- we are called to affirm that God is at work in history

God is present in other people. In Matthew's Gospel Jesus said that when we help those in need we are in fact helping him. Mother Teresa often spoke of meeting Christ in the poorest of the poor. It is a common experience of people who have given of themselves to serve those in need that they have received more than they have given.

I also believe that we discover Christ in the people who care for us. Most of us have at some time in our lives been on the receiving end of caring. We may have needed an ear to listen to our concerns or we may have needed guidance or material help. There are times someone has walked with us through the shadow of death.

Many of us have had a time when someone has said just the right word or stopped in at just the right time to lift our spirits. We have all been forgiven by someone we have deeply hurt. That is the Risen Christ present with us.

The Risen Lord is also present in the Church. Two events are closely linked in the New Testament, Jesus' return to the Father and the gift of the Holy Spirit creating the Church at Pentecost.

The Church is Christ's instrument in the world today. An early Church leader said, "No one has God as Father without the Church being their Mother." God has chosen to create the Church to be a vessel of his presence in the world. He promised wherever two or three were gathered in his name that he would be present with them. He is with us in worship, in fellowship and in serving.

The New Testament describes the Church as a body. As Ann Flint wrote:

> **Christ has no hands but our hands to do His work today.**
> **He has no feet but our feet to lead men in the way**
> **He has no tongue but our tongue to tell men how He died**
> **He has no help but our help to bring them to His side.**

The writer Philip Yancey speaks of the Ascension in these wonderful words:

> **At the Ascension, Jesus' body left the earth before his astonished disciples' eyes. But soon, very soon, at**

Pentecost, the Spirit of God would take up residence in other bodies. Their bodies.

The Risen Lord is present in and through the Church.

The Risen Christ is present in the sacrament.

Jesus comes to us at his table. The Lord's Supper is a sacrament. It is an outward sign of an invisible grace. When we eat the bread and drink from the cup in some way that we cannot fully understand Jesus is present with us in a special way.

Down through the ages Churches and teachers have tried to explain how Christ is present in Communion. These explanations are often based on the science of their day. The Roman Catholic doctrine of Transubstantiation is largely based on Aristotle's physics that dominated the science of the middle ages. Calvin and the Reformers rejected this doctrine for they realized that all attempts at explaining how Christ is present in the sacrament are doomed to failure. Yet both Luther and Calvin affirmed the truth that Jesus is present at the table.

C.S. Lewis got it exactly right when he said the command is not "Take and understand." The command of Jesus is to "Take and eat."

Christ is also present in baptism. In baptism, water is set apart for a special purpose. It becomes a sign of God's claim upon our lives. In and through water God claims us as his own.

Christ is present through the sacraments.

Finally, God is present in us. When we were baptized we received the gift of the Holy Spirit. God's spirit comes to dwell in us. Prayer and meditation help us to be open to hearing that Spirit. The Psalmist tells us "Be still and know that I am God." When we are still, when we are quiet, we can be open to the voice of God's Spirit speaking directly to us. We are spirit as well as flesh. God can speak directly to us.

The Risen Christ does make himself known through prayer. His spirit speaks to our spirit. Regular meditation and prayer connects us with the power and presence of God.

The Ascension is not an act of desertion. We are not to look back on this event in the Bible as a day of loss. It does not teach us that Jesus has left the world and can no longer be found. Rather the Ascension frees our Lord to be present with all people at all times. The limitations of the Incarnation have been overcome.

In the Wizard of Oz, Dorothy had to learn that her heart's desire was not something over the rainbow, but rather in her own backyard. So, we can learn that God has not abandoned us. He is not only waiting for us beyond the rainbow of death. Jesus is the Cosmic Christ. He is in our own backyard waiting for us. Jesus is everywhere. May we seek the presence of God in history, in people, in worship and in everyday human life. For Jesus is waiting for us. He has promised-

"Lo, I am with you always, even to the end of the age."

Questions to ponder

1. What is your mental image of the Ascension?
2. Have you ever sought to discover God at work in history?
3. Have you received Christ through care from others?

Prayer
Transcendent Jesus, you are the Cosmic Christ who is able to be present in all places and times. So often you are hidden from us. We are blind to your work in the world. Help us to overcome the blindness of our hearts that we might discover all those places you are at work in the world. Amen

Chapter XII

Christ is our Judge

**The Father judges no one, but has given all judgment to the Son.
John 5:22**

Several years ago, I did a wedding at a lake side cottage. On the way home through a small rural village I was stopped by a police officer for going 55 in a 45 mile an hour speed zone. This caused me to have to return to the town a couple of weeks later to stand before a judge and plead guilty to a reduced charge of a noise violation. I had to pay a fine and go to driving school.

This was the second time I had the experience of standing in court being accused of something. The other involved another issue of driving at excessive speed. It is interesting how vulnerable one feels when it seems all the eyes of the world are upon you. You stand before a judge who has power over your life.

This experience is a small foretaste of what is promised in the Bible. In the Nicene Creed, we declare that we believe He will come again in glory to judge the living and the dead. The Scriptures teach us that there will be a final judgment for those who have lived this life. There will come a time for each one of us to stand before a judge for a verdict on our life.

There is both good news and bad news about the promised judgment of God. The bad news is that Jesus is the judge. The good news is that Jesus is the judge.

The reality that Jesus will judge us is bad news because it means that we will be judged by his standards. Visitors to the new cathedral in Coventry, England which replaced the one destroyed by the Nazi rockets in World War II have seen a sculpture by Clarke Fitzgerald called "Plumb Line and the City." It depicts a plumb line and bob hanging over the dark city of Coventry, like the famous vision in the book of Amos. God told Amos: **Behold, I am setting a plumb line in the midst of my people Israel.**

Jesus is the plumb line by which each one of us will be judged. Our lives will be contrasted to Jesus' life on earth.

Our faithfulness to God,
Our goodness,
Our actions,
Our words
Will be compared to Jesus.
We know that we will not measure up

If we compare ourselves to politicians we can feel good about ourselves. If we compare our generosity with loan sharks we can feel big hearted. This list of people with perceived foibles is endless. If we compare ourselves with other human beings we can always find someone who puts us in a favorable light. If we set the standard low enough we can pass the test.

Unfortunately for us, you and I will not be judged by comparison with the people around us. We shall be compared to Jesus. Christ's love, Christ's faithfulness, Christ's truthfulness will serve as the plumb line by which you and I shall be measured. Jesus sets the standards by which we shall be judged. When we compare ourselves to Jesus our lives fall short.

The reality of our judgment by Jesus is bad news because everything about us will be brought into the light. The day is coming when Jesus will judge the secrets of men and women. In the final judgment of Jesus there will be no secrets. In the book of Revelation, we find these terrifying words:

> **Then I saw a great white throne and him who sat upon it; from his presence earth and sky fled away., and no place was found for them. And I saw the dead, great and small, standing before the throne, and the books were opened.**

All the truth about our lives is written in these books. All that we have said or done is recorded. All the deceitful games we have played with people, all the secret ways we have manipulated others to do what we wanted is recorded. All the harsh words we have directed at others, all the deceits we have practiced on ourselves are not forgotten.

There will be no need for a Freedom of Information Act in the judgment. Everything about us will be in plain view. The plain unvarnished truth about you and me and about everybody will be revealed.

The result of total truth will be absolutely devastating. Pascal once said that if people could know what was said about them in secret, there would not be even two friends in the world. And if men and women could know what they really looked like in the light of absolute truth there would not be one self-righteous person left.

The judgment of Jesus will be bad news, because for the first time we will see ourselves as we really are.

The judgment of Jesus is bad news, for the verdict is clear. When I went to court in that small town the outcome was clear. I knew that I had been driving 10 miles above the limit. So, in the final judgment we know the outcome. We have all fallen short of God's intentions for us. I do not think many of us would want to try and make the case that we deserve God's love and care. We understand why Paul wrote in Romans **All have sinned and fallen short of the glory of God, none is righteous, no, not one."**

Thus, there is no doubt as to our guilt. There is no hope of some Johnny Cochran convincing the judge of reasonable doubt. We can be quite certain that when we stand before Jesus his verdict is clear, guilty. The good news is that Jesus not only judges us, he also pronounces sentence. We know what we deserve. We know we do not merit the eternal love of God. Heaven is not something we have earned. Yet Jesus has promised that he has taken our punishment upon himself.

The whole purpose of the New Testament is to tell the Good News of Jesus' death on the cross. Jesus willingly gave his life as a sacrifice on our behalf. He, who knew no sin, became sin for us that we might receive pardon for our sin. Jesus' mission in the world was to bring forgiveness. John's Gospel says it best:

> **For God so loved the world that he gave his only Son, that whoever believes in him should not perish but have eternal life. For God sent the Son into the world, not to condemn the world, but that the world might be saved through him.**

The same Jesus who gave his life on the cross will be the one who stands before us in the judgment. He will grant mercy and pardon for he has already paid the price for our sin. If we trust in Jesus we shall receive the gift of eternal life. We shall enter heaven that is prepared for us.

Some may ask, that is all well and good, but how does the idea of a final judgment affect our daily actions and lives? Does this doctrine have any practical implications? The reality that we shall stand before the Risen Christ at the last judgment reminds us that our actions in this life have real meaning. What we say and do today has significance in eternity.

There was a pastor in South Carolina who was involved in the struggle for civil rights in the 1960's. One of his members came to him, very upset, to ask, why he preached so much about justice for black people. He replied, "Because I believe in the last judgment. In that day, you will know the truth. You will understand clearly that the way you treat powerless people is the way you treat Jesus Christ himself. And when all that hits you, I don't want you to look across at me, your pastor, and ask, "Why didn't you tell me? I want to be clear of your blood.'" "Do you really believe in the Last Judgment?" said the man. "Literally" the pastor replied.

I believe that He will come again in glory to judge the living and the dead. The day will come when we all shall be judged. This truth is a warning. Each action we take today will be recalled. All that we do, say and believe demonstrates either our faithfulness to Jesus or mocks him. May we ask ourselves, are we living our lives today in a way that we will be comfortable with when all is revealed before Jesus? The reality of the judgment calls on us to get our "act" right.

But our faith in Jesus' judgment is also a blessing. In the church I serve, one of the members is a Town Justice. We all know that if we are given a summons to appear in Town Court that Bob will be behind the bench. We know that Bob is an honest and kind person who will treat us fairly. It gives one a sense of security to personally know the person who sits in judgment on you.

It will be the same in the final judgment. We know who the judge will be. We will come before Jesus, the same Jesus who gave his life for us, the same Jesus who wants to live in community with us for all eternity.

So, we can look forward with confidence to that Day of Judgment for Christ has paid our penalty and will welcome us home. Judgment will become the experience of knowing the fullness of God's grace.

Questions to ponder

1. Have you ever thought of Jesus as judge?
2. What standards have you used to judge your actions?
3. What words will you say to Jesus at the judgment?

Prayer

All knowing God, we are fearful of coming before you at the Day of Judgment. We are ashamed of so many things we have done. We have forgotten so many ways that we have failed you and others. Help us to trust only in your grace and not in ourselves. Amen

Chapter XIII

The Work of the Spirit

All things I have spoken to you, while I am still with you. But the Counselor, the Holy Spirit, whom the Father will send in my name, he will teach you all things, and bring to remembrance all that I have said to you.

John 14:25-26

There is a story told about a traveling evangelist who put on quite a show. He liked to end his prayer meetings with a spectacular finish. Before the service began he would arrange for a boy to be hidden in the rafters of the ceiling with a caged dove. At the climax of his message this preacher would shout for the Holy Spirit to come down on the people, whereupon the dove was to be released and would fly over the heads of the people.

One night at the end of his exhortation he shouted for the Holy Spirit to come down and nothing happened. Again, he raised his arms and shouted, "Holy Spirit descend on your people." Again, nothing happened. In the expectant quiet the little boy poked his head over the rafter and called down, "A yellow cat ate the Holy Spirit, should I throw down the cat?"

In this chapter, we mark a major transition in our study of the creed. We began with a focus on the first article of the creed which talks of God the Father. Then we moved on to the second article which speaks of God the Son. We now transition to the final article that speaks of the work of the Spirit. Together we proclaim **we believe in the Holy Spirit, the Lord and giver of life.** So, in this final article of the Creed we will explore the role that the Holy Spirit plays in our lives. The work of the Holy Spirit is to make God real to us.

I think that sometimes our understanding of the Christian faith appears to assume that the cat has eaten the Spirit. For the Holy Spirit is frequently absent from our approach to God. We do not always recognize how central the Spirit is to the Christian faith.

Sometimes the Spirit appears to be tacked on to the faith, or merely a part of our baptismal formula or the ending of prayers.

In the book of Acts we are told that the Holy Spirit came upon the disciples in the Upper Room. For a period of forty days following the Resurrection Jesus appeared to them. Then we are told Jesus ascended to the Father. It was only after the Ascension that the Holy Spirit came upon them. The Holy Spirit came to give the disciples a continuing sense of the presence of God.

The work of the Holy Spirit is to make God real to us today. The Holy Spirit gives life to our faith. It is the Holy Spirit that gives us experiences of God's direction, comfort and presence in our lives-now-today.

Historically, the Church has been somewhat scared of the Holy Spirit-and for good reason. We must acknowledge that most of the great errors committed by Christians through the ages have been made by men and women who have claimed that they had a special gift of the Spirit.

In the second century church, there was a man called Montanus. Montanus claimed that the Holy Spirit spoke through him. He claimed that the Spirit had told him that the New Jerusalem had already come and was located in what is now a part of Turkey. People followed him to the location and started a community. They developed a heretical form of Christianity that lasted for some time.

Similar movements have come along all through Christian History. Remember some twenty odd years ago the tragedy in Waco. David Koresh claimed that the Spirit of God was speaking through him in a unique way. Koresh was able to convince others of the authority of his leadership. They started a new community that rejected much of our culture and led to a deadly confrontation with the FBI.

While it can be dangerous to over emphasize the Holy Spirit, it is just as fatal to neglect the role of the Spirit, for it is the Holy Spirit who makes our faith real. It is the Spirit that enables us to sense the reality of God in our lives.

I believe that often our experience of the Christian faith is like walking down the main street in a movie or TV set. If you walked down Main Street of the set you might see a bank or grocery store or a school or a church. They all appear to be real.

But the minute you try to walk into the bank, or buy groceries or enter the school or worship in the church you discover it is only a fake town. It only appears to be real. It's all painted plywood and foam. The town is merely a set director's trick to make us think we are in a real town.

Our faith in God is frequently like the Hollywood set. We go to church, we sing the hymns and we recite the creed. We do many of the things which would make us appear Christian. But the minute we are tested, our faith is found wanting. When we are tempted, when a loved one dies, when we lose our jobs, when someone needs our help, then we react in the same way as non-believers around us.

When our lives as Christians are put to the test, so often the unreality of our faith shines through. The shell of our pretense is shattered. It is then that we wonder why? Why is my faith in God not more real?

The Hollywood Set has something to teach us. From the street these buildings look real, but they lack one thing. They lack depth. They are only two –dimensional buildings. They have width and height, but they lack depth.

Our faith is similar. When you and I recite the creed, we say that we believe in the Father, Son and Holy Spirit. Each person of the Trinity adds a dimension to our faith. When we ignore the Spirit, our faith lacks depth.

This does not mean that our faith is untrue. We say we believe in the Father –maker of heaven and earth and of all that is seen and unseen. That is a true statement

We say that we believe in Jesus Christ who suffered for us under Pontius Pilate. That is a true statement. We believe that Jesus died on a cross outside Jerusalem. His sacrifice means that our sins are forgiven and our place in heaven is secure.

Often that is as far as we go in our understanding of our relationship with God.

Yes, we believe that God created the universe way back then.
Yes, we believe that Jesus died for us nearly two thousand years ago.
But what about today?
What about now?

Our faith often lacks vitality because we do know where God is today.

Too often we do not allow the Holy Spirit to play a role in our lives. Ask yourselves this question. If all mention of the Holy Spirit were not to be found in the Bible would it make any difference in how we live? Often our answer would be no.

Our faith lacks vitality and reality when we ignore the Holy Spirit. For the unique role of the Holy Spirit is to make God real to us. In his book **A Theology of Pastoral Care,** Eduard Thurneysen describes the Holy Spirit in this way.

> **The Holy Spirit is indeed no other than God himself approaching us and grasping us; he is our God, the God acting with us and in us through his Word and choosing us to be his Children. God is the Creator and Father over us; in his Son he is also with us, and in the Holy Spirit he is in us, to open our eyes and ears so that we learn to recognize love, and fear him as our Father in his being with us in the Son.**

The Holy Spirit makes God real in our lives. The Holy Spirit gives life to our faith. That is clearly the message we hear in the second chapter of Acts. In this passage, the followers of Jesus are gathered in the Upper Room. They seem to be frightened and without direction or purpose. Remember most of these people had known Jesus in the flesh. They had heard him preach. They had seen him heal people. They had experienced Jesus being betrayed, arrested and put to death. Many of them had seen and heard the Risen Jesus. This gathering had experienced the Risen Christ directly, but now this was in the past. Jesus had changed their lives, but that was in the past.

Now they were huddled in the Upper Room unsure of what was next. They did not know God's place in their lives.

Then we are told the Holy Spirit came upon them. It was the Spirit that transformed these timid disciples into apostles who went to the ends of the earth sharing the good news of Jesus. The Holy Spirit gave courage and direction by mediating God's presence to his people.

The coming of the Holy Spirit made God real to his disciples.

Jesus said in the Gospel of John that it was good for him to go away in order that the Holy Spirit, the Counselor could come. If you sat down and made a list of all the things the Bibles tells us that the Holy Spirit does for us you would be amazed. In Corinthians, we are told that preaching, teaching and healing are gifts of the spirit. In Romans, we are told that it is the Spirit who teaches us to pray. In the Book of Acts the Spirit continually guides the disciples. Indeed, we should call Luke's second book the Acts of the Holy Spirit.

The Holy Spirit makes God's presence manifest in our day-to-day experience. The power of the Spirit is available to each one of us. We do not need to receive the Spirit, for you and I have been baptized in the name of the Father, Son and Holy Spirit. We do not have to go looking for the Holy Spirit for it is within us.

The question becomes how do we become open to the work of the Spirit in our lives? I would offer three simple steps.

First, we begin this process by wanting God to become more real in our lives. This starts with our admitting that our faith lacks depth. God is not always real in our lives. Jesus can sometimes seem remote from the everyday struggles of our lives. Yes, he has assured us of our ultimate destiny, but he seems disconnected from our work, our relationships and our recreation. If we confess that God is not at the center of our daily life, we begin to seek the presence of the Spirit.

The next step is to take at least ten minutes each day seeking God. Set a time convenient for you. Be still, mediate, pray, read Scripture- seek to be open to God's presence. If we follow that discipline yearning for the presence of God, the Holy Spirit will begin to speak to us. We will begin to feel God's presence.

The third step is even more difficult. We must be willing to take risks to follow the leading of the Spirit. When we are open to the work of the Holy Spirit, the Spirit will begin to nudge us to change our lives. If we are truly to grow in faith, you and I have to take the risk of following that leading. We will have to act when we are not sure if what we are sensing is the Holy Spirit or our own unconscious.

If we begin to be open to the work of the Holy Spirit we begin an adventure with God in the here and now. Our lives become a journey with God. The presence of the Holy Spirit can infuse our lives with meaning, direction and joy.

The work of the Holy Spirit is to make God real in our lives. The Spirit brings us peace, joy and fulfillment. May we begin today to seek a deeper experience of God. May we allow the Holy Spirit to breathe energy into our relationship with the divine that we might learn to serve Jesus more fully.

Questions to ponder

> 1. Does God sometimes seem disconnected to your everyday life?
> 2. Have you ever considered the role of the Holy Spirit?
> 3. What risk might you take in following the lead of the Spirit?

Prayer

Loving Spirit, so often you seem far away from us. You seem like a God more of the past then the present. Teach us to explore God the Holy Spirit. Help us claim the promises of baptism and so have a deeper experience of your presence in our lives. May we follow the leading of your Spirit. Amen

Chapter XIV

Spoken Through the Prophets

> **Keep these words that I am commanding you today in your heart. Recite them to your children and talk about them when you are at home and when you are away, when you lie down and when you rise.**
>
> **Deuteronomy 6:6-7**

As we learned in the last chapter it is the work of the Holy Spirit which makes God real to us. One of the ways God reveals himself to us is through Scripture. The Creed tells us that the spirit has "spoken through the prophets." The Bible is God's self-revelation through the inspiration of the Holy Spirit.

In our passage from the Book of Deuteronomy we are reminded of the important role that Scripture is to play in our personal and corporate lives. The words of the Bible are to shape our common life. These passages do not speak of the Scriptures as an abstract rulebook we are to look to when we get into trouble, but rather as a part of everyday life that functions to mold our hearts and minds.

While the Bible has served as the central authority of Christian life and unity, it has also been a source of disunity as well. Scripture can be used for good or ill. Remember in the story of Jesus' temptation the devil uses words of Scripture to tempt Jesus. It was this incident that Shakespeare may have had in mind when a character in *The Merchant of Venice* says **the devil can cite Scripture for his purpose.**

In almost every age the disagreements within the Christian Church have involved how we should approach Scripture. Reflecting on these battles throughout history, the great Danish philosopher Soren Kierkegaard once suggested that Christians should gather all the Bibles in the world on one small island. They then should set the pile of Bibles on fire and as they burned all should pray, "Lord take them back for we do not know how to use them."

Yet if we are to grow spiritually, the Bible must play a central role in nurturing that growth. I would like us to reflect on how you and I ought to approach the Holy Scriptures.

I would like to begin with several mistaken ways men and women approach the Bible.

First the Bible is not to be an object of worship. I believe that there are times when people approach the Bible as something that we ought to idolize. I have heard people say, I do not need creeds, I do not need the church, I believe in the Bible.

Yet we are called to believe in Jesus not the Bible. Remember there was a community of faith before there was a New Testament. After the resurrection, the early Christians believed in Jesus. They did not have any of the Gospels or Epistles to read. Yet the Christian faith was still strong and growing because they knew the story of Jesus' death and resurrection.

The books of the New Testament were written to record the events of Jesus' life and pass them on to those who would come later. The Bible is not an end in itself. The Bible is a means to an end, and that end is a relationship with the living Christ. God has given us the Scriptures as a tool. They are a tool for us to use to discover Jesus and his will for us. The Bible is not to be worshipped but rather used to discover Christ. As I Timothy tells us **All Scripture is inspired by God and is useful for teaching the faith and the correction of error**

Another mistaken approach to Scripture is to consider all parts of the Bible to be equal. While the entire Bible has some value, not every part of the Bible is of equal value in teaching the faith.

Is there anyone who would deny that the first chapter of John, which teaches that the eternal word was made flesh, is more important than a chapter in Leviticus that gives directions for keeping a kosher household?

Would anyone maintain that the obscure passage in Genesis which talks about the sons of God intermarrying with the daughters of men, that no scholar can really comprehend, is equal to Paul's hymn of love in I Corinthians 13?

Can anyone doubt that the first three chapters of Genesis which teaches us about the meaning and purpose of creation are not vastly more important than the Book of Esther which does not even mention the name of God?

It is clear that there are parts of the Bible that are more important than others. If we read the Bible to encounter Christ, then we should read more of the New Testament than we do the Old, and more of the Gospels than we do the Epistles.

What then is the proper approach to the Scriptures? The primary function of the Bible is to teach us about the nature of God. You and I are to approach the Bible seeking to find God. The nature of God is not self-evident. God is outside this created order. Since he is not part of the created order there is no human faculty, which enables us to discover him. Yet the hidden God, through the work of the Spirit, has revealed himself to us through the Bible. It is the record of God's interaction with his people.

Recall for a moment the over-all flow of the Bible. The Old Testament begins with the creation of the world. We are told why God created human beings and what our purpose is in the world. It describes our sinful nature. It moves to the story of Abraham who is called to form a new nation. Moses saves the people from slavery in Egypt and leads them to the Promised Land. We learn how the nation of Israel grew and prospered under King David and how the nation was unfaithful to God and how the prophets continually called the people back to faithfulness. We are told how the people began to look for a Savior.

The New Testament tells the story of Jesus. We are told of his life, death and resurrection. The story is then told of how the church spread the story of salvation into the world.

The story of God's love for us is what the Bible is all about. Thus, the first questions we should ask when we read the Scriptures are:

What does this passage say about God?

What do these words reveal about God and his relationship with me?

A second approach to the Scripture is to read seeking direction for how to live our lives. The Bible teaches what we should do in our lives and it does this in several ways.

The most obvious way is with rules. The Ten Commandments are the primary example. God has revealed his will that you and I are to live by. Some of these rules guide our relationship with God. Others, such as the commandment to not steal, helps us to live in community.

A second way the Bible sets the direction of our lives is through models. If we wonder how to pray, we can look for models in the book of Psalms. There are Psalms for people who are joyous, others for people who feel guilty, for others who feel defeated. There are Psalms which reflect almost every human condition. These can serve as models for us.

There are human models in the Bible as well. The Bible is full of stories that record the experiences of men and women seeking to be faithful to God. They are shown with all the shortcomings and failings as well as their victories. We can learn from the examples.

Thus, a second set of questions we are to ask when we read a passage of Scripture include:

What does this tell me about how I should live my life?
What change does God want me to make?

There have been many battles down through the years fought over the Bible. The Scriptures have been used and abused by people trying to bully others. People have used proof-texts to hit each other over the head.

Yet when all is said and done,
After all the arguments have been made
What really matters is reading the Bible for ourselves.

No matter what we may say we believe, if we do not read the Scriptures then they do not function as an authority in our lives. Our approach is far less important than contact with the Word itself.

If our Bibles remain sitting on the shelf or coffee table they may look nice, yet they have no impact on our lives. We need to read the Scriptures. Many may find the Bible to be intimidating and believe that it can only be read by experts. The truth is the Scriptures are for everyone. Gregory the Great wrote:

> **Scripture is like a river broad and deep, shallow enough for the lamb to go wading, but deep enough for the elephant to swim.**

If you have not read much in a long time, please begin by reading one of the Gospels. Focus on Matthew, Mark, Luke or John for a period of time.

Read short passages at a time and then ask yourself two questions, What does this reveal to me about the nature of God? And then, how does this teach me to live my life now?

If we become faithful, regular readers of the Bible, I know that we will be led ever closer to God. The Holy Spirit will do the work of making God real to us. The Scriptures will begin to shape how we think and who we are. If we meditate upon the Scriptures, they will bring us into the very presence of God and allow it to shape our hearts and minds. We should approach the Bible expecting it to shape our very souls.

In our approach to the Bible we trust in the work of the Holy Spirit and so we pray, "May the same spirit that inspired these writers to record these words interpret their meaning to our hearts and to our understanding."

Questions to ponder

> 1. Have you ever made the mistake of making the Bible an idol?
> 2. Do you read the Bible for information or transformation?
> 3. Can you commit yourself to regular reading of Scripture?

Prayer

Life giving Spirit, help us to accept the gift of the Scriptures that you have given to us. Remind us that they are not a weapon for us to use in correcting others, but rather an aid for our own transformation. Give us hearts open to receiving the gifts that the Bible seeks to give. Amen.

Chapter XV

One, Holy, Catholic and Apostolic Church

I tell you, you are Peter, and on this rock I will build my church, and the powers of death shall not prevail against it.
Matthew 16:18

But we have this treasure in earthen vessels, to show that the transcendent power belongs to God and not to us.
II Corinthians 4:7

There is a Presbyterian minister who tells a story about his experience in leading a congregation in Tennessee. Each Sunday one young man would come through the door following worship and have something negative to say about the sermon. It did not matter what the subject might happen to be he would make some derogatory remark. One Sunday he said, "That's about the sorriest sermon I ever heard."

The next Sunday he came through the line and said, "Do you call that a sermon?" The third Sunday he said, "That is about the nearest to nothing in a sermon I ever heard."

The minister became so upset that he took it to a Session meeting. He said, "Ladies and Gentlemen, every Sunday this man has some negative comment to make about my preaching, I do not know what to do?"

One of the elders replied, "Oh, don't pay attention to him. He's just mentally very slow. All he can say is what he repeats from other people."

This story reminds us that the church is an institution made up of human beings with all the faults and blemishes that people have. Thus, it can be somewhat of a shock for us to recite in the creed that we believe in **One Holy Catholic and Apostolic Church**.

I have often been asked why do we Protestants affirm that there is one Catholic Church? After all, there seems to be so many different churches and often there is not a lot of oneness found in them? We are not catholic.

One of the great saints of the church I serve was named Betty Hazer. Betty used to tell a wonderful story that answers these concerns. Many years ago, Betty and her husband Art were asked to be best man and matron of honor at the wedding of his cousin. The wedding was to be held in a Roman Catholic Church. During the rehearsal, a relative of the bride who thought she should be in the wedding party, continually kept pointing out to the elderly Priest that Betty and Art were not "catholic" At the first instance the Priest ignored her remarks. But after she continued to interrupt the Priest became increasingly annoyed.

Finally, after one final reminder he spoke sharply to the woman. He reminded her that all Christians are part of the Catholic Church. Catholic means universal. He then told the woman not to speak of herself as Catholic but in the future to call herself a Roman Catholic.

This old priest knew better than most of us that God has created a universal church that is to be united in love. We are to be one in Christ. Yet often our witness is stifled by the divisions of all the Christian denominations that dot the landscape. These are the result of ancient fights among Christians. They are a living testament to our lack of unity.

I believe that God is going to hold us accountable for the divisions found in his Church. For we have allowed human weakness to divide the Catholic Church. Jesus calls on all people to love one another, yet we cannot even all worship together.

When we proclaim that we believe in one Catholic Church we are not saying that we believe in our own home congregation. We are not professing allegiance to our particular denomination. We are affirming the reality of Christ's church around the world and across time and space. We believe that the Church of Jesus is made up of all those who seek to follow Jesus.

You and I are to welcome all who share faith in Jesus as companions in faith. We are to seek common ground with all Christians around the world. If real peace and understanding are to be found in the world it must start with Christians reaching across culture, geography and language to fellow believers. We believe in a universal church called to be one around the world.

We also affirm that the church is to be holy and apostolic. We sometimes hear this to mean that we are to be perfect little saints who act like the first followers of Jesus. Holy does not mean perfection. Holy means to be set aside by God for a purpose. In Matthew Jesus proclaims **I tell you, you are Peter, and on this rock I will build my church, and the powers of death shall not prevail against it.** Peter is holy because God calls him for a purpose. Peter is the first member of the Church which Jesus created to take the Gospel to the world.

Peter was the first of what Paul called "earthen vessels" to hold the gospel. Peter was not chosen because he was perfect. He was an earthen vessel. He was a human being who failed Jesus in his time of crises. Peter was quick to anger and he would change his opinions with the blowing of the wind. Yet Jesus was able to use him to begin his church. Peter helped to share the story of Jesus around the Roman world until his martyrdom in Rome.

Since the time of Peter, the church has held the treasure of the Gospel in earthen vessels. When we declare our faith in a Holy Apostolic church we are not claiming that the church is pure, spotless and without blame. The church is an earthen vessel. It has made and will continue to make mistakes.

It is important for us to admit the earthiness of the Church. The church has had episodes of shameful behavior during the years. In almost every Christian tradition there were times when Jews were persecuted. There have been times where the Church was used to promote a political agenda or for personal gain. The Church in America was largely silent on the issue of slavery in our early days. The Church is fallible. Christians are fallible

Yet Jesus seeks to build a universal church for a purpose. God used earthen vessels to share the good news of God's love with the world. Down through the centuries despite its failings, the church has been an earthen vessel that contains the treasure of God's love.

Some of you may have heard the story of Reynolds Price. Reynolds Price was a novelist who taught at Duke. He died in 2011. Price was a man who believed in Christ but was alienated from the Church. In an interview, he once said:

> **I've never felt it was wrong of me not to belong to a church. Sometimes on Sunday mornings I do wish I were in some nice church, listening to music and taking communion. But I don't want to hear a sermon about how to repair the church's roof, or to be asked to coach the boys' soccer team or come to the men's Sunday night supper.**
>
> **I've always rejected two things about the church in the parts of the world where I've lived. The first is that the Protestant Church was the nerve center of racism throughout my childhood and young manhood. The other is the degree to which churches now, and perhaps many synagogues too, are little more than social clubs for their members. I have friends who are at church five nights a week-it's their social life. I don't condemn that, but it's the last thing on earth I want of the church.**

This quote points out clearly the failures of the Church. He highlights many errors that we should be concerned about in our common life. Yet Price's words also contain another message. It is clear he was a person of faith. He believed in God, he trusted in Christ. He hungered for the sacrament. For the truth is he learned about God in Sunday school and worship in his childhood church. He was introduced to the good news of Jesus in the same church which acceded to racism. The goodness of God was able to break through the brokenness of the human institution. The gospel came to him through; an earthen vessel.

Remember that a wooden manger in Bethlehem was chosen to hold the word of God incarnate. An ordinary young girl named Mary was chosen to give birth to the word made flesh. In like manner, God created the Church to be the vessel which contains the continuing presence of Christ in the world.

God created the Church to be nothing less than an instrument of grace. That is what holy means. The Church is an earthen vessel through which God reaches into this world. It is the faithfulness of men and women through the ages which has allowed us to hear the "Old Old Story of Jesus and his love." Persecution, corruption and evil have not been able to destroy the human vessel of the church in order that Christ might be known.

Jesus told Peter that he was going to build his Church on him. Jesus was going to use normal human beings for an extraordinary purpose. God has continued to use his Church to bring people to him. In baptism, you and I have been made part of that earthen vessel full of grace.

It is the same with the Lord's Supper. At the table, we receive simple elements from the earth. These every day basics of bread and cup are used by God to come to us. Jesus seeks to feed us with his presence and love. So, we come as flawed, imperfect people to be used by God for his purpose.

Friends, no matter how flawed-I believe in the Church of Jesus. Christ has created his church to incarnate his love and share it with the world. I believe in one holy catholic and apostolic church.

Questions to ponder

> 1. Does the word Church have positive or negative connotations for you?
> 2. How broad an understanding of Church do you have?
> 3. Can you accept the earthiness of the church?

Prayer

Community building Lord, we thank you that you have called each one of us to be part of your community of faith. Help us to see beyond the flawed human institution some sign of your kingdom. May the grace, which flows through the earthen vessel, which is the church, spread into the broader world. Amen.

Chapter XVI

The Gift of Forgiveness

Happy are those whose transgression is forgiven, whose sin is covered.

Romans 4:7

One of the primary gifts of the Spirit is the experience of being forgiven. We declare that we acknowledge one baptism for the forgiveness of sins. In these words, we are reminded of the centrality of grace in our faith.

The great novelist Robert Louis Stevenson is quoted as having once said. **"There is nothing but God's grace. We walk upon it; breathe it; we live and die it; it makes the nails and axles of the universe."**

The grace of God is a central message of the Christian Faith. We believe that God loves each human being. That love is expressed in creation. God's grace sustains human life. It was made manifest for us in the incarnation of Jesus in the world. The grace of God was demonstrated in fullness in the Cross of Christ.

I believe that grace is made most evident in our day-to-day lives through our experience of forgiveness. Jesus came into the world to make it possible-

For our sins to be forgiven
For our brokenness to be made whole
For our hurts to be healed.

When we declare that we believe in the forgiveness of sins we are claiming our faith in God's grace working in our everyday lives.

In the Gospel of John, we see this grace at work in the life of Peter. There is this wonderful appearance by the Risen Christ in which he shares his love and grace with the one who had denied him.

In this story, the Risen Christ meets the disciples on the beach early in the morning. After the crucifixion, several of the disciples went back to their normal lives. Peter and others went back to their regular jobs as fishermen. These followers of Jesus had spent all night fishing without catching anything. They came to the shore and found the Risen Jesus preparing breakfast over a charcoal fire. The fire is a key to understanding the story. Remember only a few short days before Peter was standing around a fire while Jesus was being tried. Three different people came up to Peter and asked him if he was a follower of Jesus. Each time Peter denied that he knew Jesus.

Now several days later Peter comes ashore to discover Jesus standing by a fire. There is no way that Peter could not have faced Jesus without remembering his failure. After they had finished eating their breakfast, Jesus turned to Peter and asked, "Simon son of John, do you love me more than these?" Peter answers," Yes Lord you know I love you." Jesus then says, "Feed my sheep." A second time Jesus asks, "Simon son of John, do you love me?" Again, Peter answers, "Yes Lord, you know that I love you." Jesus said to him, "Tend my sheep." A third time Jesus asks, "Simon son of John, do you love me?" One can almost sense Peter's hurt and frustration when he responds "Lord you know everything-you know the ways I failed you. You know my night of defeat, you know my sin- you know all of that and yet you know that I love you." For a third and final time Jesus tells him to feed my sheep.

This encounter with the Risen Christ tells us several truths about the nature of the forgiveness that Jesus gives to us.

First it teaches us that Jesus did for Peter what Peter could not do for himself. Peter could not lift the burden of guilt from his own shoulders. Peter could not undo his denials. The only way for Peter to find healing was for him to experience forgiveness from the one against whom he had sinned.

This was the same experience of grace that led to the Reformation. Martin Luther became a monk in order to please God. Luther would often have bouts of depression in which he would feel unworthy of God's love. He would throw himself into becoming a perfect monk. He fasted more than his brother monks. He prayed and studied more than others in his order. He drove his confessor crazy with his need to confess every fault. His confessor at times wanted to hide from him. In short Luther spent years seeking to become a person worthy of Christ's love and acceptance. Life for Luther was a burden and struggle.

Finally, after many years of study of the Scriptures, Luther came to rediscover a truth of the Gospel. Human beings cannot make themselves worthy of God's forgiveness. We cannot do anything to make up for our sin. Our weakness is not overcome by human effort.

Luther came to realize that God comes to us in Jesus to offer us forgiveness. Grace comes as a gift from a loving savior. It is Jesus who paid the price for us to make grace possible. The Risen Christ came to Peter and offered reconciliation and forgiveness. So, Jesus offers forgiveness freely to us each day of our lives.

Secondly this story teaches us that forgiveness gives us back our future. Forgiveness is not about the past. Forgiveness does not erase the damage our sins have done to others. The hurts we have caused by our errors do not evaporate. Forgiveness does not mean the past is cancelled.

Peter could never wipe away the memory of his night in the courtyard when he denied that he even knew Jesus. The forgiveness David experienced after his encounter with Nathan did not undo the damage his failure had caused. His adultery with Bathsheba was still a fact. Bathsheba's husband Uriah was still dead. The damage caused by his sin was not undone.

Forgiveness does not change the past, but frees us for the future. It means that we no longer are imprisoned by our past. Forgiveness sets us free to fulfill the calling God places on our lives.

The Risen Christ came to Peter and restored him. When Jesus said, "Feed my sheep." It was like saying, "Peter, here is your old job back again. Here's your calling, given back to you fresh, clean and new. Go ahead; fulfill your calling, Feed my sheep."

The truth of God's forgiveness means that your future and mine is open. We are not trapped by what we have done in the past. Our lives are not predetermined by the mistakes we have already made. The grace of Christ frees us to move into the future with the possibility that we might become the men and women God has called us to be.

Arthur John Gossip, a former professor at the University of Glasgow tells of an experience that he had during the First World War. There was a young soldier in his battalion who had messed up an assignment and been court-martialed and punished for it. When he returned to duty, Gossip recalls the commander of the battalion saying, "We must show him we still trust him or the lad will go to pieces." Not once, Gossip relates, was the incident alluded to. A few weeks later, the commander put the young man in charge of his company in a very difficult situation- the same company in which he had previously failed. Within a few days during which he fought a grim battle, the young man had proven himself worthy of the task. Honor after honor was bestowed on him along with a field promotion. "What else could I do?" He told the chaplain, "I failed him and he trusted me."

The forgiveness shown by the commander gave the soldier back his future.

It is possible for me to face the future because I believe in the forgiveness of sin. God's grace works much like a water treatment plant. There are sewer lines all over the county. These lines take all the dirt and sewage that we human beings produce in everyday life. All these pipes lead to the treatment plant. Through filters, chemicals and other processes the treatment plant takes the impurities out. The pipe at the other end of the plant empties purified water back into the river.

In a similar manner, God's grace takes the failures, weaknesses, and sins of our lives and filters them out and removes them that we might begin anew each day. Each time we confess our faults the loving Christ cleanses us and restores us to his presence. I would find life very difficult if I had to carry the burden of all the sins I have ever committed. If all my failures, weaknesses and errors were always present with me it would be impossible to function. But the grace of Christ takes it away and allows us to start anew.

You and I have a continuous need for the forgiveness that only Jesus can give us. Each week that we worship we participate in an act of confession. We share with God all our shortcomings and failures of the week. We cannot wait to hear the gracious words declared in the pardon: Friends believe the good news of the Gospel in Jesus Christ you are forgiven.

Thinking about the story of Peter and Jesus on the beach, I became aware that most people are more familiar with the story of Peter's denial of Jesus in the courtyard than they are with his forgiveness by Jesus around a fire on the beach. We know the story of Peter's sin better that we do the story of his forgiveness.

I believe that this may be the case because it is easy to identify with Peter's failure. Each one of us finds it easy to understand Peter's weakness. We have all failed Jesus ourselves many times in our lives. We have all been unable to live up to our own standards, much less the standards we think God has for us. We all know we are sinners.

What is harder for us to believe is that forgiveness is possible. Lent is over; we are to move from the darkness in the courtyard to the new morning on the beach where Jesus offers forgiveness and new life.

In times of great doubt, when struggling through dark periods of his soul, Martin Luther would sometimes touch his forehead and say to himself, "Martin, be calm, you are baptized." In times of doubt, inner turmoil, hopelessness and confusion, we too would do well to touch our foreheads, where the sign of our baptism was made, the baptism which reminds us of God's grace and forgiveness.

I believe in one baptism for the forgiveness of sin,
That forgiveness begins when we confess our sin,
Acknowledge our fault
Recognize our need
And turn to the Risen Christ.

There is nothing we can do to earn that grace; we simply turn to

Jesus in love.

Remember there is only one question that Jesus asked Peter. "Do you love me?" and there is only one question that Jesus asks us, "Do you love me?"

If you love Jesus, forgiveness comes as a free gift, a gift that makes a joy filled life possible.

Questions to ponder

> 1. Has someone ever forgiven you and it felt like you had been given your life back?
> 2. Does guilt keep you from moving on in your life?
> 3. What makes it hard to accept forgiveness?

Prayer

Merciful God, you are more willingly to forgive than we are to ask. Help us to accept your grace and so be able to move forward in love. Amen.

Chapter XVII

Life in the World to Come

Then I saw a new heaven and a new earth; for the first heaven and the first earth had passed away, and the sea was no more. And I saw the Holy City, the New Jerusalem, coming down out of heaven from God, prepared as a bride adorned for her husband; And I heard a loud voice from the throne saying, "See, the home of God is among mortals. He will dwell with them and they shall be his peoples, and God himself will be with them.

Revelation 31:1-3

In this chapter, we come to the final clause in our study of the Nicene Creed. We have slowly worked our way through this basic statement of the Christian faith that is shared by almost all followers of Jesus across time and space. We move to the final phrases of the Creed which point to our eternal destiny. We affirm that we look for the resurrection of the dead, and the life of the world to come.

The text for this chapter is from the book of Revelation. This is one of the more difficult books to comprehend. One of my professors at Princeton Seminary used to say, "**The Fathers of the Church did not want the book of Revelation included in the canon because it would be misused by fanatics and history has proved them correct.**"

Revelation is a book full of symbols, images, and pictures, which are not always, clear in meaning. This has allowed all kinds of religious zealots to interpret this book in their own way. This book is so full of strange images that one wonders how to approach it. Yet I assume that most people are curious about heaven. We want to know what it will be like when we die. We wonder what eternity will be like. The Bible does not give us a great amount of information about the nature of eternal life. The Scriptures are not a guidebook written by a traveler who has visited heaven and is reporting all that she or he has seen and experienced. The writer of the Book of Revelation was given visions concerning the reality, which we call heaven. In this chapter I would like to share several truths about heaven revealed in these visions.

First, this text teaches us that heaven is radically different from this life. We read **Then I saw a new heaven and a new earth; for the first heaven and the first earth had passed away, and the sea was no more.** Heaven is not merely a perfected form of life on earth. It is a new reality different in quality not just quantity from this existence.

All too often when we attempt to think about heaven, we merely think of what gives us pleasure in this life and then magnify it in order to produce our image of what heaven will be like.

Several years ago, an article appeared in the **Wall Street Journal** that talked about the beliefs of Palestinian Moslems on the West Bank of the Jordan. It seems that almost everyone who dies is soon proclaimed a martyr to the faith in its battle with Israel.

The article included this paragraph:

> **It is easy to see why martyrdom is so coveted. For Muslims, there is no higher honor. According to Islamic belief, a martyr goes straight to paradise, where he sits next to God, is absolved of all of his sins and enjoys 70 virgin brides.**

In this off-putting quote, we find an example of an attempt to make heaven satisfy an earthly fantasy of some young males. Almost each one of us could design our own idea of heaven from favorite earthly experiences.

But the book of Revelation teaches us **Then I saw a new heaven and a new earth; for the first heaven and the first earth had passed away, and the sea was no more.** Heaven is a completely new reality. It is not just more of now. It is not a place where we get to do everything we want to do. That is why the writer of the book of Revelation uses strange images and pictures.

In the Gospel stories of appearances of the Risen Jesus this is also made clear. The resurrection is not resuscitation. It is a very new type of body that Jesus has. The disciples do not always recognize him. He moves quickly about. Easter does not promise just more of this life.

Secondly, at the center of the reality of heaven is a relationship with God. In this life, we seldom have complete experiences of God's love. Much of the time, God seems to be a hidden God whom we can only know or experience fleetingly. A full experience of the presence and love of God is at the core of heaven.

This is a central part of many images of heaven found in the book of Revelation. There are images of choirs gathered around God's throne. We are told that the Lamb of God is in the midst of people. In a variety of ways and in a number of pictures we are given the message again and again that: **I heard a loud voice from the throne saying, "See the home of God is with mortals. He will dwell with them and they shall be his peoples and God himself will be with them**

The promise of heaven is that we will know completely the full love of God. We shall live in his presence and know the joy, acceptance and love that only he can give us. All the problems, hurts, sins, and suffering of this life will be put behind us and we will experience the joy prepared for us from the foundation of the world.

Paul's great chapter on love in I Corinthians recognizes the heavenly nature of love. He reminds us that love never ends. All the other things in life will pass away, but love will remain. The one thing we can take with us into eternity is love. We can experience it now partly, but then he said we shall know love **face to face.**

While we cannot fully understand what heaven will be like because it is a new reality, we do experience intimations of eternity in this life. We can have brief experiences of what heaven will be like.

The experience of beauty can give us a taste of heaven.

There is a wonderful legend about how Christianity came to Russia. The story is told that in 987, Prince Vladimir of Kiev sent ambassadors to the Moslems, the Jews, and the Latin Christians in Rome and to the Orthodox Christians in Constantinople in order to choose the best religion for his people. The report that the envoys brought back about their experience in Constantinople made the Prince decide without hesitation that his nation would follow Byzantine Christianity. The ambassadors reported on their experience in Hagai Sophia in these words:

> **We did not know if we were in heaven or on earth for on earth such beauty is not to be found. We thus do not know what to say, but we know one thing for sure. God dwells there among men.**

It was the beauty of the worship experience that transported their souls into God's presence.

There are many experiences of beauty in this life that can give us a glimpse into heaven. Beauty can be found in the natural world. The Created order can strike us with a wonder which points beyond itself to eternity.

The arts, painting and music can help us have a foretaste of heaven. Beauty not only points to God, it can be a source of contact with God himself.

Human love and friendship can be an example of heavenly love in human life. An example comes from the experience of the poet W.H. Auden:

> **One fine summer night in June 1933 I was sitting on a lawn after dinner with three colleagues, two women and one man. We liked each other well enough but we were certainly not intimate friends, nor had anyone one of us a sexual interest in another. Incidentally, we had not drunk any alcohol. We were talking casually about everyday matters when, quite suddenly and unexpectedly, something happened. I felt myself invaded by a power, which, though I consented to it, was irresistible, and certainly not mine. For the first time in my life I knew exactly- because, thanks to the power, I was doing it- what it means to love one's neighbor as oneself. I was also certain, though the conversation**

continued to be perfectly ordinary, that my three colleagues were having the same experience. (In the case of one of them, I was able later to confirm this.) My personal feelings towards them were unchanged- they were still colleagues, not intimate friends- but I felt their existence as themselves to be of infinite value and rejoiced in it.

I recalled with shame the many occasions on which I had been spiteful, snobbish, selfish, but the immediate joy was greater than the shame, for I know that, so long as I was possessed by this spirit, it would be literally impossible for me deliberately to injure another human being. I also knew that the power would, of course, be withdrawn sooner or later and that, when it did, my greed and self-regard would return. The experience lasted at its full intensity for about two hours when we said goodnight to each other and went to bed. When I awoke the next morning, it was still present, though weaker, and it did not vanish completely for two days or so. The memory of the experience has not prevented me from taking advantage of others grossly and often, but it has made it much more difficult for me to deceive myself about what I am up to when I do?

This experience was for Auden an intimation of the love we will experience in its fullness in heaven. **Behold the dwelling place of God is with me. He will dwell with them and they shall be his people.**

I believe the experiences of beauty and love in this life serve as foretastes of heaven. They give us hope and faith for eternity. These experiences can help to guides us towards our heavenly home. We can rejoice today, for Jesus has prepared a place for us in his kingdom where we shall experience his love and presence in its fullness.

When we say We Believe, the Nicene Creed unites us with every Christian around the world today and every believer who came before us who now surround the throne of heaven. In this life, we know in part, but then we shall know fully the truth of the words from Revelation. **"Behold, the dwelling place of God is among mortals. He will dwell with them and they shall be his people."**

Questions to ponder

> 1. Do you think of heaven as more of the same or a completely new reality?
> 2. What intimations of heaven have you experienced?
> 3. What hopes do you have for heaven?

Prayer

God of the future, our lives are in your hands. We trust you in life and in death. Give us signs of your kingdom in this life that we might live in hope. We trust that in eternity we might know the fullness of your love. Amen

Chapter XVIII
Conclusion

The Nicene Creed has served the universal church well for almost 1700 years. The Creed does not give every detail of our faith. For example, it touches very little on the earthly ministry of Jesus. But it does guide us towards the great mystery of Jesus.

The purpose of this book is to begin a discussion and not to give easy answers. In the first five hundred years following Jesus' death, Christians wrestled with many basic teachings of the faith. The Ecumenical Councils came together to struggle with important questions. The Orthodox Bishop Ware talks of this process in these words:

> **Secondly and more important, the councils defined once and for all the Church's teaching upon the fundamental doctrines of the Christian faith-the Trinity and the Incarnation. All Christians agree in regarding these things as 'mysteries' which lie beyond human understanding and language. The bishops, when they drew up definitions at the councils, did not imagine that they had explained the mystery; they merely sought to exclude certain false ways of speaking and thinking about it. To prevent people from deviating into error and heresy, they drew a fence around the mystery; that was all.**

This is a very important point. Most of early Christian doctrine does not attempt to explain all truth, but rather points in the direction where truth might be found. It is like a treasure map. We won't dig over there because there is nothing to be found. The map tells us to start digging around the x for that is where truth resides. This means we do not have all the answers but are on a journey together to discover truth.

I hope this book serves as one interpretation of the treasure map which is the creed. I invite you to not just read the creed, but rather to include it in your prayers. In prayer, it can become a pathway into the heart of God.

www.ingramcontent.com/pod-product-compliance
Lightning Source LLC
Chambersburg PA
CBHW070117080526
44586CB00013B/1319